LIFEBLOOD II

How Owners Who Survived

Will Thrive in the New Economy

by

Sam Frowine

Institute
FOR ENTERPRISE BUILDERS

Published by the Institute for Business Owners
122 St. Albans Lane Suite D
Davidson, NC 28036

Printing History

Edition One, June 2006

Edition Two, January 2013

ISBN: 1482502585

Lifeblood II: How Business Owners Who Survived Will Thrive in the New Economy

Dedication

To my wife, Velda,

and to my children

Leslie, Sam, Molly and Andrew

In loving memory

of my dad and mom, Sam and Janet

Acknowledgements

Every day of my business life, I come along side business owners who are on the journey of ownership. I am thankful to these owners who have allowed me to partner with them as their advisor, coach, mentor and friend. Their willingness to share candidly with me their vulnerabilities, their hopes, their fears, their discoveries and, sometimes, their raw exposure to harsh new financial realities has motivated me to update this book. The lessons and lasting truths that are revealed in trials are often the most enduring ones—-that's what my mom used to say. The years since 2008 have afforded business owners a lot of trials to test our principles, beliefs and convictions. I am grateful for the many owners who have allowed me to learn from them and to tell their stories through my work.

Lifeblood II would not have happened without the constant persistence of Peg Robarchek, my business writing soul mate. For more than twelve years we have written hundreds of publications, a handful of books and thousands of documents that, today, make up my digital library, found at SamFrowine.com. Her contributions reflect the smarts of a journalist and the wisdom of a person who cares deeply about people and the importance of private enterprise in America. We come at life from very different angles, but our convergence of thought is uncanny. I am grateful for all the ways that the creative tension of our partnership contributes to the quality of my writings.

SEF

Author Biography

Working with business owners to achieve their goals is Sam Frowine's passion and his purpose, with the common theme of navigating healthy business adaptation in an ever-changing world.

For more than 25 years, he has been owner, CEO, managing partner or investor in more than a dozen enterprises—several very successful and a few not so successful. Sam is also the author of the *Biz Prophet* column in **Greater Charlotte Biz Magazine**, the *Business Wealth* column in **The Charlotte Business Journal; 40 Profound Concepts that Will Inspire Your Business Journey; Blueprint for Building Great Enterprise**, and **Foundations for Great Enterprise & True Wealth.**

Sam is founder and owner of The Performance Group, Performance Capital Group and the Institute for Business Owners. Sam holds a doctorate degree in developmental psychology from the University of Cincinnati, where he was a faculty member for seven years. He received his undergraduate and Master of Science degrees from Ohio State University. For more information, visit www.samfrowine.com

Table of Contents

Introduction to the Second Edition   xvi

Introduction to Edition One   xx

Cracking The Business Wealth Code

Part One

Restoring Economic Health: 1

Chapter One   3

Business Ownership: Staying in the Game

Chapter Two   17

Playing the Asset Builder's Game

Chapter Three   33

Your Vision, Your Money

Part Two   45

Fundamentals

Chapter Four   47

Smart Money Rules

Chapter Five   51

Learn to Earn

Chapter Six   65

Eyes on the Money

Chapter Seven   77

Make Cash Flow

Chapter Eight   87

Avoid the Debt Sinkhole

Chapter Nine   99

Hedge Your Bets

Chapter Ten   111

Leverage Down

(Continued)

Chapter 10   123

Think Like a Capitalist

Chapter 11   137

It's Fundamental: A Legacy of Hope

Appendices   147

The Asset Builder's Code
The Language of the Asset Builder
Sam's Bookshelf

INTRODUCTION
TO THE SECOND EDITION

To prepare for the new edition of **Lifeblood**, which was first published in 2006, I took a deep dive into the lives of business owners. I had a compelling sense that there was a need to hear their views on ownership in the changed economy.

One of those owners was Dennis[1], a serial entrepreneur who recently acquired an underperforming technology company.

Dennis has been a loyal reader of my work for years. We've corresponded, but never met face to face, so I was looking forward to meeting him. Like many of the owners I work with every day, Dennis was a golf-shirt casual kind of guy. He led me into an unpretentious and informal conference room that doubles as a place where colleagues and clients share lunch.

A systems-minded owner, Dennis is a success story. He had just turned the corner in his recently-acquired business. He wanted me to know that he had relied on the fundamentals expressed in his dog-eared copy of **Lifeblood** to get there.

But it was clear, after he showed me the copy of **Lifeblood** that he keeps in his desk drawer, that Dennis had something more on his mind.

---

[1] Except where full names have been used, names of owners and some of the details of their businesses have been changed to preserve confidentiality.

"Please don't tell me you're coming here to say that the fundamentals you wrote about in *Lifeblood* have changed," he said, "because I live by that book."

What he really wanted to hear, of course, was that there are some things we can hold true and believe in, especially in this time when everything seems so uncertain.

When *Lifeblood* was first published, business owners operated within a different economic reality. It's reasonable to suppose that the rules of the ownership game would have changed for this new day. That's why I decided to update and revise the book. But as I carefully re-read it, I realized that, while our circumstances have changed, the rules of the game have not.

What in the world can owners find to believe in and operate by in a book that pre-dates the downturn by more than two years?

Peter Drucker could've told me: *Fundamentals, Sam. Fundamentals.*

When author Peter Drucker died in November, 2005, hardly a national business magazine failed to speak to the wisdom of this iconic business guru who had written more than 39 books. But the wisdom from which I took comfort, the legacy he passed to me, was this: *Business fundamentals never change.*

And so it is with the Seven Smart Money Rules at the core of *Lifeblood.*

The first edition of *Lifeblood* spelled out the Seven Smart Money Rules that I had observed and codified after twenty-plus years of business ownership and business ownership consulting. Those Seven Smart Money Rules, prior to 2008, formed the foundation for the principles and practices I taught about business ownership wealth.

My takeaway as I've re-examined my work with owners since the 2008 economic meltdown is that *economic circumstances may shift with the times, but deep economic truths never change.*

The Seven Smart Money Rules are as relevant today as they have ever been—and more critical than ever for owners to understand and implement. They encapsulate the fundamentals that Peter Drucker taught us.

In fact, as I think about my experiences with business owners in recent years, I would say that those who had been operating by Smart Money Rules pre-2008 were better positioned to withstand the crushing blows of the tectonic shift than those who had not. And that's where I find hope for those of us who are still standing, those of us who are rebuilding and those of us with our eyes on the future.

As part of the preparation for updating this book, I've been very intentional about interviewing business owners across the country, as well as gathering their thoughts through surveys and my daily conversations.

Why do their opinions and insights matter? Because the health of our society is entwined with the health of business ownership.

There's not a business in these times that hasn't had to adapt or reinvent its business model significantly. There's not a business owner who hasn't been challenged to persevere when giving up might've seemed simpler—even, at times, a relief. But let's admit it—no, let's *claim* it—business owners will be around when everything around us has passed away. Business owners are the cockroaches of the economy. You can stomp on us, but you can't kill us.

Yes, we're tired. Tired to the point of fatigue. And at times we feel discouraged. But we're still in the game.

And if you're still in the game—either in the same company you've been in for years or in some new incarnation—you are a winner. You are successful. You're part of an entrepreneurial revolution being fought to protect our economic freedom, individually and in our communities. Your contribution to the economic value of our nation makes you—makes each of us—a winner.

So *Lifeblood: How Successful Business Owners Achieve Wealth* has become, in this new edition, *Lifeblood II: How Owners Who*

Survived Will Thrive in the New Economy. In it, I hope, you'll find encouragement in knowing that the game may change, but the rules still apply. Success lies not in learning new rules, but in adapting these enduring fundamentals to the new playing field.

Recently, my wife, Velda, had outpatient surgery. Pretty quickly after she came out of recovery, a nurse brought her a cup of water with ice. It had been hours since Velda had water and she drank it like someone coming out the desert.

The nurse smiled and said, "Some things just taste extra special when they've been taken away."

So it is for me as I re-examine the fundamentals of business ownership during our nation's time in the economic desert. I am refreshed, my hope renewed. There is water in the desert. Drink with me.

Sam Frowine
January 2013

Author's Note: It's against my nature to repeat anything, but I hope you'll reread the original introduction to **Lifeblood** *with fresh eyes, as I have, to see what perspective we can gain from the past. Although some of the details and statistics may have changed, I stand by my optimism for the potential of business ownership expressed in this original introduction written in early 2006. For many, this degree of optimism may not seem realistic; don't believe it. These principles are still the foundation for healthy business ownership economics today and they will be tomorrow.*

INTRODUCTION to the FIRST EDITION
CRACKING THE WEALTH BUILDER'S CODE

No one—**no one**—is in a better position to tap the wealth potential of the 21st Century economy than business owners.

It's been a long time in coming, but entrepreneurs are now recognized as the backbone of the U.S. economy. But recognition and respect are secondary to the fact that business owners now have the greatest potential for significant wealth simply because they are players in the number one game in town.

That's the good news.

Here's the bad news: Too many business owners will lose this opportunity—the very opportunity they've created for themselves and others—because they haven't learned the rules of the Business Wealth Builder's game.

You and I and the other 25 million-odd business owners in the U.S. [2] are leaders in the revolution that will re-invent and reinvigorate our economy and, along the way, provide us with unprecedented opportunities to build significant wealth.

In his books *The Millionaire Next Door* and *The Millionaire Mind*, Tom Stanley offers plenty of research to prove that self-employed people— entrepreneurs like us—are far more likely to be millionaires than those who work for others. Our dogged determination makes us winners. Stanley

[2] The Small Business Association, Office of Advocacy, 2006

reports that 26 % of the deca-millionaires (people with a net worth of $10 million or more) he studied were business owners; one in three of the millionaires were business owners. Others were retirees (many of whom had once been entrepreneurs), professionals, CEOs of major corporations and those who inherited their millions. In his first study, he found that of the 80% of millionaires who were still working and not retired, more than two-thirds were business owners.

We're definitely in the right game.

But hold on. Don't get too heady. As with most euphoria, there's a dose of reality around the corner. This dose is sad: most of us will fall on the battlefield of the Entrepreneurial Revolution.

About 600,000 businesses fail every year. And every year, 600,000 optimistic entrepreneurs start new businesses. Of the businesses that manage to keep their doors open, only about 4% will ever top $1 million in revenue. With every financial milestone—$5 million, $10 million, $20 million—the percentages drop.[3]

I know the fears and I know the uncertainties. I'm a business owner—to be exact, I own four of them at the moment.[4] My wife, Velda, says I'll own businesses until the day I die. I can't argue with that.

I've been a business owner for more than 20 years. I've been in manufacturing and I've been in service industries. Like every other business owner I know, I've sweated payroll, struggled to hold the line on overhead and stared at the ceiling in the middle of the night with revenue on my mind. I still do. Like a lot of business owners, I've bought and sold and turned around businesses. I've walked away from some of them with only the few dollars I needed to start over; others, I've sold for a return on my initial investment that ranged from adequate to satisfying to significant.

Inevitably, I start another business. I'm an entrepreneur; what else am I going to do?

[3] Ibid.
[4] As of 2013, my most current business entity is SamFrowine.com, an electronic community and an elibrary of resources for business owners.

When I started out, it was no badge of honor to be a business owner. I think it broke my mom's heart.

"Why can't you be like Joey?" she said when my old friend became an optometrist. "His mother's so proud."

In my first jobs, I was a prison social worker, then a day care teacher. I earned a doctorate in developmental psychology and graduated to teaching University of Cincinnati students how to think. My mother was proud of me then. I wasn't exactly an optometrist, but at least I had "doctor" in front of my name.

But a university is no place for the entrepreneurial spirit.

I wanted to run my own show. Control my own destiny. And put some food on the table while I was at it—always a challenge on a professor's salary. Besides, I didn't like playing by anybody else's rules. I could always see a better way of doing things, but nobody in academia was interested.

So I thought up an idea for a business. I didn't get rich, but I did find a life-long passion for the art of business ownership.

Nobody's going to mistake me for the Donald Trump of small business, but I have walked the owner's walk for decades. I've owned or invested in businesses in home building materials, manufacturing, printing, marketing and trade show exhibits. I've learned about distribution, production, human resource management. I've learned about business planning and forecasting.

I've also learned that none of those factors is the key to controlling my own destiny. The key is found in the art of business ownership as the vehicle for building wealth.

Since 1994, my consulting company has worked with the owners of closely held companies to optimize the wealth-building potential of their enterprises. We've built a model for achieving profitable and sustainable growth specifically tailored to the unique circumstances of private enterprise. So I work in the trenches every day with owners who are fighting to beat the odds. I've seen my share of business owners who are hanging on by a thread or churning money to keep the machine running or wrecking their lives on the brutal and unforgiving treadmill of business ownership.

I've also seen the owners who cross the chasm from start-up to sustainable, legacy-bound enterprise. They hit the $5 million mark or the $15 million mark. They expand or acquire or franchise. Some of them achieve financial independence. Those who cross that chasm seem to have found the formula for economic freedom. They belong to a different breed of owners.

Although I'm interested in all shapes and sizes of owners, I'm most interested in those who have found the key to building sustainable business wealth. I call them Wealth Builders.[5]

What do they know that the rest of us don't know?

For the last four years, I've written about the Wealth Builders' mindset, their decision-making process, their beliefs and values for *American City Business Journals.*[6] I tell the stories of owners and their stories reveal the roots of their successes—and the failures that have made them stronger. Their stories demonstrate the distinctive traits and characteristics that show up again and again in the men and women who have built significant wealth on the platform of private enterprise.

For two decades, I've been refining and integrating the best of these practices of highly successful business owners into a body of knowledge for business owners who desire to become Wealth Builders. This body of knowledge has become the Business Wealth Builder's Code; it separates the winners from the also-rans. The Code is based on the hard-earned wisdom of experience. My own, yes, but it's also drawn from all the business owners I've met over the years. Every one of them has contributed to the depth and breadth of the body of knowledge that makes up the Code.

[5] In this Second Edition, I have shifted to the language of Asset Builder to reflect changing priorities and definitions for success. Even at press time, the change leaves me conflicted because I still believe that business ownership is the best pathway to build wealth and a significant legacy.

[6] The *Business Journal* column ran for more than five years and is still available online by doing a byline search for *Sam Frowine*. In addition, *Greater Charlotte Biz* magazine has published my *Biz Prophet* column since 2009.

The Wealth Builder's Code is not a simple how-to. It is not a step-by-step formula. It is a creed that anyone can adopt. It's less prescription than perspective shift. The Wealth Builder's Code affects the ways we orient to our role as business owners. It reveals a pathway for developing a powerful leadership model, a company culture that supports wealth-building principles, excellent execution against the strategies that lead to enterprise success and, ultimately, to greater economic success.

But most significantly, the Wealth Builder's Code shapes the business owner's beliefs and values about business ownership. It becomes a way to redefine ourselves as business owners who are elevating entrepreneurship to the status of leaders and innovators in the 21st Century economy.

My mother, by the way, walked through my business recently and gave it her blessing. Like the rest of the world in the 21st Century, she had come to esteem business owners and their significant role in our economy as never before.[7]

The first critical component of the Wealth Builder's Code is adopting a new perspective and new practices around the resources of time and money. Time, money and people are the lifeblood resources of every business.

Lifeblood. Sounds heavy-duty. Exaggerated, maybe.

Don't kid yourself. ***Lifeblood is the difference between the businesses that open their doors tomorrow and the ones who don't.*** Lifeblood is the difference between the mom-and-pops that never get ahead and the enterprises that cross the chasm and become economic machines.

Lifeblood is the business owner's lifeline.

Lifeblood is found in the relationship between time and money: Healthy and rhythmic cash flow buys time to refine the success formula of the business. Long-term, significant success occurs through mastering the

---

[7] Janet Frowine passed away September 13, 2009.

game of protecting the lifeblood of the business. We do that by first recognizing that every decision, every choice, impacts the lifeblood of the business.

Sound pretty basic? A no-brainer?

Then why do the majority of business owners never master it?

This book focuses on what the Wealth Builder's Code tells us about the lifeblood resource of money.

Money: When we've got it, we've bought the time to survive another day. When we're out of it, we're out of time.

Money: It's the way we measure success and the way we measure failure.

Money: Most of us know more about how to get our hands on it than we know about how to keep it and grow it. Some of us know less about money than we know about anything else in our business.

But all of us, no matter what life stage our business is at, no matter what industry, no matter what our long-term objectives, can achieve greater success when we operate by the smart money rules that Wealth Builders use in their journey to economic freedom.

Welcome to the journey.

Part One

Restoring Economic Health:

The Fundamentals of Asset Building

The Asset Builder's Code

Making money is hard;
hanging onto it is even harder.

CHAPTER ONE
BUSINESS OWNERSHIP:
STAYING IN THE GAME

"Where'd the money go?
You know—the cash left over after all the bills are paid."

We've all heard the stories. If you're a business owner, you probably have one of your own. The marketplace is over-inventoried with post-meltdown stories about business owners who were forced to the edge of the abyss and survived…or didn't.

I remember one of my dark days, a day that sums up the meltdown for me: January 5, 2012.

One of my companies expected to close any day on the sale of a business we were representing. The deal was pivotal to the 2011 economic success of my company, in which I was an investor with a significant stake. Our company had worked the deal for three years—three of the toughest years in which I've ever navigated the sale of a business asset. When the deal closed, our fee would give us breathing room.

Then it happened. Unexpectedly and beyond anyone's comprehension, the deal fell apart.

It fell apart for reasons symptomatic of this epic time. Buyers got cold feet. Bankers got spooked. The seller got anxious as the deal dragged on and revenue in the asset declined week by week. Yet I continued to expect the deal to close because the buyer had already invested more than half a million dollars in legal fees. And because I didn't want to consider the consequences to all my companies if it didn't.

By 2011, the small-to-medium-sized companies that are my consulting company's bread-and-butter were hurting. Many that had survived were battered and bloodied, worn out and worn down. They all needed our advisory services, and checked in with us regularly. But more and more often they were taking our advice and cutting all but the absolute essentials from their budgets—including, sometimes, the services of my consulting firm.

That's just smart fundamentals. Maybe.

But our consulting company bottom line, from time to time, looked anemic. Accustomed to operating without debt, we had tapped a few lines of credit to get us over a hump here and there. Plus, we had used a chunk of our available capital to buy out a partner who needed to move on. We weren't going down—thankfully I had diversification in my ownership portfolio and flexibility in my overhead. But I wanted us out of debt. My portion of the payout from closing the deal in the other company would accomplish that.

Then, at the eleventh hour, the deal fell apart. A mid-six-figure payday, vanished. That hurts any day. On the back end of my toughest year of business to date, January 5, 2012, felt like Black Thursday.

Within seven days, two long-term clients declared they weren't able to meet their obligations to us. And a long-time employee broke his non-compete to start his own practice.

Dang! It was an unraveling that was beyond my anticipation.

Fast-forward to the end of 2012 and my ownership landscape looked friendlier. Despite these stability-threatening tremors—or maybe *because* of them—I implemented more changes in my consulting firm. We've gone virtual and digital. We've reduced the costs of fixed overhead by 90%. And I've shifted focus to something that's been part of my long-range vision even before technology offered a way to do it—I've created an electronic library of tools and materials for business owners under the brand SamFrowine.com.

The flexibility and responsiveness we had built into our systems, plus processes for adaptive thinking and accountability, equipped us to survive a major blow. The changes have been daunting, but I feel lighter and more free than I've felt in four years…five years…no, ten years. Maybe forever. I feel like I've experienced deliverance. Not because we're out of the woods—I'm not sure how any private enterprise can consider itself completely secure in today's economy—but because I'm operating from Smart Money Fundamentals as I pursue what I'm called to do. It gives me confidence and peace to be playing my game smart.

But enough about me. This is about you!

War zone

We've all seen or been part of more dramatic stories than mine, of course. I've seen sell-outs for pennies on the dollar. Tens of millions lost in a single enterprise. Industries dry up and assets change hands. I've seen owners who were closing in on retirement face the reality that the exit door is closed indefinitely if not permanently. I've seen thriving service businesses with teams of technicians stripped back to their one-man-and-a-truck start-up status. I've seen business owners cry amid the wreckage and others protect their resources while maneuvering around the bodies displaced by the new economy.

Most of us are tired to the point of exhaustion. We've experienced a level of stress greater than we ever imagined. Some of us are living with the kind of post traumatic stress that follows time spent in a war zone.

But we're still here.

In surviving to play the game another day, most of us have harvested some fundamental lessons and plan to apply those lessons to our next entrepreneurial venture. Some of us have kept our doors open continuously and haven't missed payroll…yet. Some of us are mean and lean. Some of us have been in the fortunate position to gather in assets others could not sustain. All of us have a heightened perspective on the value of the business asset we own.

Forget the statistics

In the first edition of **Lifeblood**, I started out by affirming something we all knew: Business ownership is risky. It's a high-stakes game and historically many entrepreneurs lose their shirts. Everybody knows that, and the marketplace has proven it in a big way since 2008 – from 2007 to 2010 the small business failure rate increased by 40%.[8] Small business bankruptcies increased from just over 19,000 nationally in 2006 to more than 60,000 in 2009.[9] In addition, some sources indicate that business ownership of companies that offer employment could be at an all-time low.

Those numbers are sobering and humbling .

I suggest we forget them.

> **The Owner's Voice***
>
> *"Although there is uncertainty more than ever, I feel the basics of free enterprise are well when you are blessed to have a good product and are in a growing industry."*
>
> *This quotation and subsequent quotations were taken from comments made by respondents to Sam's 2012 survey of business owners and their perspective on the current state of the economy.

Unless you plan to be part of those statistics in the near future, I suggest we pay attention to different numbers—the day-to-day numbers where we find the story of the lifeblood of our own businesses. It is not SBA statistics that determine our success; it is determined by the lifeblood of our businesses. That is a fundamental truth of business ownership.

The winning numbers

Ask a business owner how his or her business is different now than it was pre-meltdown and virtually all of them will mention fundamentals—

---

[8] Dun & Bradstreet, The State of Small Business Post Great Recession, www.dnbgov.com
[9] U.S. Small Business Administration Office of Advocacy

they talk about the money, time and relationship capital that add up to what I call the Lifeblood of a business.

Some of them will tell you they're more immersed than ever in the sales process. Some will tell you about the radical moves they've made to contain overhead or shift to a variable-based compensation model or create an out-of-the-box solution. They talk about the scarcity of outside capital—sometimes cursing their tight-fisted bankers or laughing at the irony of the phrase "relationship banker." They talk about revenue and margins. They can recite their numbers by heart.

Business owners today are riveted on the fundamentals.

How those fundamentals of money, time and relationship capital play out will be different from business to business, from industry to industry. But the principles behind those fundamentals do not change. No matter how different the game seems, the fundamentals never change.

And when we practice the fundamentals, we can win the game.

How we define a win may have changed, too. But we can increase the odds of winning by sticking to the fundamentals that protect the lifeblood resources of our businesses.

Lifeblood Plus

Redefining the win

In today's economy, even our definition of winning may be different.

Once upon a time winning meant being the biggest, growing the fastest, acquiring the most. Those are accomplishments, not wins.

People are coming to a new understanding of what it really means to win the ownership game. Winning today starts with finding the contribution that enables us to be profitable enough to stay in the game, which then gives us the time, money and relationship capital to make a difference.

Winners pay attention to the fundamentals not because it's important to beat the competition or even earn our way onto a Fast 50 list. Winners pay attention to the fundamentals because that's what keeps us in the game.

Fundamentals that protect the lifeblood resources of a business build the foundation for success.

Where's the money?

Long before the economy collapsed, business owners came to me almost every day asking essentially the same question: *Where'd the money go?*

Sales were good and revenue was up, so why were they struggling to make payroll? If business was so good, how did they get to be so cash poor? *Where'd the money go? You know—the cash that's left over after all the bills are paid.*

In many cases, the money was going out the back door while they were paying attention to all the wrong metrics. Their eyes were on what was coming in, and if that looked good, they relaxed. When times were good, it was easy to let the fundamentals slide. They had bought into the delusion that revenue equaled wealth.

Then the economy crashed and the owners who hadn't paid attention to the fundamentals were among the first to fall. *Where'd the money go?*

Making money has always been hard. Holding onto money has always been hard. Acquiring liquid cash has never been harder. As owners, every decision we make about the resources of our businesses impacts our cash flow (liquid cash), which is the most critical lifeblood resource of our business.

Lifeblood Plus

How challenging has the economic picture been since 2006? Let's look at statistics on business bankruptcies.

According to the U.S. Census 2012 Statistical Abstract, business bankruptcies numbered 19,695 in 2006; 23,889 in 2007; 33,822 in 2008; 55,021 in 2009; and 59,608 in 2010.

The American Bankruptcy Institute reports the following numbers: 19,695 in 2006; 28,322 in 2007; 43,546 in 2008; a peak of 60,837 in 2009; 56,282 in 2010 and 47,806 in 2011. Lower numbers continued to be reported in each of the first three quarters of 2012; if Q4 in 2012 matched the Q4 2011 numbers, the total would be 8% lower than the previous year.

Neither of the sources cited here differentiate between private enterprise and publicly-traded entities.

The Owner's Voice

"The headwinds facing business owners is substantial. I honestly feel that the importance of entrepreneurship is missed by most governmental, banking and funding resources. At the end of the day, we do what we do despite the infrastructure and not because of it."

That fundamental bears repeating: *Liquidity is the most critical lifeblood resource of our business.* That has not changed.

The business owners who practiced that fundamental, and the other fundamentals we'll cover in this book, were on more solid ground before the crash. They are the ones who are still in the game today.

Freedom. Legacy. Dignity.

It would be disingenuous of me to tout business ownership as the fastest and surest pathway to disproportionate wealth today. But I do see cells of opportunity where owners can continue to secure economic freedom while building a personal legacy. Business ownership in America remains the greatest vehicle for achieving freedom in the world.

Economic freedom. Personal legacy. Autonomy with dignity. These are some of the most powerful motivations behind ownership.

Even in these challenging economic times, I haven't met a single business owner who is ready to go to work for somebody else.[10] Most of us believe we'll find a way to make it work until the day we don't. We believe we can write our own script and make our mark on the world and that conviction is one of the last things we'll give up. Freedom and legacy.

As owners of private enterprises, we're willing to stake everything we own or hope to own for the chance to create economic freedom. Even a seriously weakened economy hasn't dampened our enthusiasm for entrepreneurship. The meltdown raised awareness that entrepreneurs play a significant role in the nation's economic freedom. Although we have real

---

[10] In all of our surveys, we did receive one response from a former business owner who claimed to be happier receiving a corporate paycheck. I haven't met him and, much like the Loch Ness Monster or Bigfoot, I will not be convinced this owner exists until I talk with him face to face and hear that he is truly content with the trade-off. Strange and unexplainable things do happen.

9

confidence issues right now, I've never seen owner pride greater than it is today among those who are still hanging in and surviving. It is a different kind of pride, too, not born out of hubris but out of the humility of having faced down conditions we could not control. Almost like survivors of a natural disaster.

One of the most successful owners I've had the privilege to know over the last decade has a poignant story of what it is to come through one of ownership's toughest decisions with his dignity intact.

Wayne's[11] company is one of the most respected brands in a regional market. The company has been around for a couple of decades and is a top earner with loyal, repeat customers. At its peak, prior to 2008, the business employed more than 100 well-paid people and had locations in multiple cities.

Despite the growth, Wayne remained a hands-on, passionately involved owner.

For the first few years of the recession, the company felt the pain of the downturn. But it was such a healthy business that everyone remained confident in the early days that it would still be standing when the economy revived. By year three, the economy was gasping for air and Wayne's business was limping. He started to feel strangled by the exposure of a personal estate that was deeply entwined in his business.

Closing the doors and losing everything had become a very real threat.

After giving it the good fight for almost four years, Wayne accepted a roll-up offer from a major corporation. It was the best pathway he could see to save the jobs of his 100-plus employees. He is now a top executive in the board room of the behemoth that swallowed his business, watching from a front-row seat as the company culture he created is dismantled.

Outwardly, Wayne holds his head high. But the choice that strengthened the company and provided security for his employees feels like an ach-

---

[11] Except where full names are used, names of owners and some details of their companies have been changed to preserve confidentiality.

ing personal loss for this owner who falls into the category of the best of the best enterprise builders.

My prediction is that, in time, Wayne will walk away from the business he once founded. The entrepreneurial spirit that is his core will find a way to reinvent itself.

American idols

As far back as 2005, a **New York Times** story by Elizabeth Olson stated, "With corporate greed and boardroom scandals long in the headlines, entrepreneurs are swiftly replacing corporate titans as America's business idols."

Lifeblood Plus

Defining Money Choices

Business owners face choices that impact the lifeblood of the business every day. An owner's choices in four key areas may reveal telltale signs that the owner doesn't understand how to play smart.

Ownership reward: Will ownership fund a lifestyle either by unreasonably high compensation or by charging off as "business expenses" such high-priced toys as cars, boats, beach houses, thus sending the message to the organization that it's okay to squander resources?

Compensation model: Will the business reward based on performance, establishing a modest pay base for employees with incentives for achieving clearly -defined objectives? Or will the business create an entitlement mentality with 1) higher base compensation; 2) the expectation of holiday bonuses and annual raises regardless of the financial state of the company; 3) failure to instill in company leaders a sense of ownership for financial results.

Internal profit centers: Will each department or division be held accountable for financial success by tracking revenue and expenses directly related to that department? Or will all revenue go into one big pot, making it difficult if not impossible to determine where the revenue is coming from and where profit leaks may be hiding?

Capital planning: Will ownership view the business as an asset to be invested in? Will ownership plan for the day when outside capital may be required, either through loans or outside investors?

Owners like Wayne probably don't feel like heroes; if ownership today were a televised reality show, they might feel more like the ones who just got voted off. But in the aftermath of 2008, Olson's statement in the **New York Times** article still seems prophetic to me.

The economic crisis stirred up fears of economic instability. Americans wondered what would save them. The most common answer was entrepreneurship—the hundreds of thousands of entrepreneurs who hang out their shingles in cyberspace or rent the storefront on Main Street. We're no longer the guys who couldn't snag a job in corporate America. We could be the protectors of America's economic freedom. That's a legacy most of us never anticipated.

Freedom and legacy.

Even in today's economy, those opportunities still exist.

The Owner's Voice

"It is riskier to work at the whims of another."

Seizing them will mean operating by the fundamentals. Gone is the day when there's a margin for financial messiness and failure to implement the fundamentals. Those who do not live by the fundamentals will not remain in today's game. The competition will wipe them out, if they don't wipe themselves out first.

Who's going to survive? You? Me? The guy around the corner who's outfitting his home office and praying he's got what it takes?

Here's who will survive: the ones who **master the rules for protecting the flow of liquid cash as if it is the lifeblood of our businesses**. Because it is.

Show me the money

I don't know about you, but I'm obsessed with money. I don't know a business owner who isn't. (Even the ones who say they aren't.)

We wake up thinking about money. We measure every opportunity on how much revenue it will generate. We squawk about every dollar spent in our organizations. We don't count sheep in our sleep, we count receivables. Even if money isn't our number one motivator, we all reach a point in the life of our businesses when money is the first thing on our minds when we wake up and the last thought drifting through our brains when we fall asleep at night.

Based on the experiences of the owners in my world, money is precisely what business owners **should** obsess about.

When we've got money, we're still in the game. When we don't have money, it's game over.

Today, having money translates into cash on hand. Liquidity. It always did. That's a fundamental. But in the days of easy credit, some of us dismissed that fundamental as the old way of doing business.

A Dun & Bradstreet report[12] from some years ago listed 14 common causes for business failure; the most common causes could be traced back to money. They centered around pricing, lack of capital, debt, lifestyle expenses and lack of knowledge about financial record-keeping and decision -making. A **New York Times** article from early 2011 reinforced the same idea: six out of ten reasons for small business failure were directly related to money, from the price tag for over-expansion to the lack of a cash cushion to operational inefficiencies like paying too much for rent, labor or materials.[13]

Translation: Business owners who fail have made mistakes around money. They didn't make enough. They spent too much. They spent it on the wrong things or at the wrong time. The lifeblood of the businesses—cash on hand—dried up. It all came down to money.

Sooner or later, no matter what our motives or dreams, the reality of business ownership is this: *If we're not in it for the money, we won't be in it for long.*

For all of our obsessing about money, it's harder than ever to know exactly how to be good stewards of the money that does come in. With so

---

[12] "Small Business: Preventing Failure—Promoting Success," Lewis A. Paul Jr., Wichita State University Small Business Development Center
[13] "Top 10 Reasons Small Businesses Faill," Jay Goltz, New York Times, January 5, 2011

much uncertainty, do we continue to invest in the health of our companies and hope the investment pays off, even if that payoff is farther down the road than ever? Do we scale down our dreams? Is economic freedom still a possibility and, if so, how is it different today? And what about our legacy? How much of our dream can we walk away from before we've abandoned our legacy altogether? Can we make all these adjustments and still maintain our dignity and our autonomy?

We all have a lot of questions and there aren't any easy answers. But I do know where the answers are found: In the fundamentals.

For more than a decade, my own enterprises have offered resources for business owners who wanted to cross the chasm that separates the great idea from the great enterprise. Both face-to-face and digitally, we give owners tools to build infrastructure and organizational structure and leadership capabilities. We help them develop strategy and untangle problems. We sell businesses. We introduce investment capital. Oh, and another not-so-minor matter—we help companies implement disciplined financial reporting.

In other words, we offer the fundamentals to business owners who are at a crossroad where decisions must be made and change is inevitable. More than ever before, that crossroad marks a place where owners want to know, *Where's the money?* Their customers have squeezed the margins out of the business. Banks have called their lines of credit. They're living with a distinct sense of vulnerability that comes with knowing that cause and effect today is arbitrary and beyond their control. *Where's the money?*

If answers are scarce, we still have plenty of choices. And every choice we make comes back to the lifeblood of our companies.

Ownership Perspective

1. Why did you decide to become a business owner?

2. Do you keep a record or journal about the lessons, questions or insights derived along your journey as a business owner?

The Asset Builder's Code

*Every decision, every choice, impacts
the lifeblood of the business.*

CHAPTER TWO
PLAYING THE ASSET BUILDER'S GAME

"We're business owners. We do the impossible every day."

Business owners are a different breed.

We want the freedom to control our own destiny. We don't want anyone telling us what to do. Never tell us we can't, because we'll always find a way. And we won't play by anybody's rules.

We're cowboys.[14]

Wondering what's over the next hill and how to get there is in our blood. Our land was settled, in large part, by men and women with the courage to cross an ocean that extended farther than the horizon. Our very form of government was conceived by visionaries who inspired a ragtag bunch of farmers to take on one of the greatest military powers in the world. Our nation spread from one sea to the other because of men and women who wanted the freedom offered by open spaces and ungoverned territories. Driven by an adventurous spirit, these pioneers transformed into entrepreneurs who figured out how to do things others believed could not be done, or things no one else ever dreamed of. We rode in horseless

---

[14] I know, I know. Cowboy is a gender-specific term. And whenever a man talks about gender issues, he risks putting his foot in his mouth. So let me acknowledge that, yes, I believe entrepreneurs have what I call a cowboy spirit—a certain confidence in their walk and a lone-rider attitude. And I see that cowboy spirit in almost every owner I encounter—even the men.

carriages. We flew. We made the remarkable and the impossible common-place—telephones and televisions and computers and space travel and a World Wide Web for instantaneous communication.

That same spirit of adventure flows through our veins today. It's a spirit that never goes away. We're entrepreneurs, waiting to unleash our energy and imagination at the right time.

Times like these.

The double-whammy

How will we use our pioneering nature in these extraordinary economic times?

The entrepreneurial mindset has long been a cornerstone in the foundation of our country. If ours is indeed the land of opportunity, most

---

Lifeblood Plus

Revolutionary Numbers

Entrepreneurs are the 21st Century pioneers who will redefine our economy. Those are bold words. The facts behind them are even bolder.

- 20.9% of new ventures in 2011 were launched by people 55-64; in 1996, that demographic launched 14% of new companies (American Express Open Forum blog Entrepreneurship: The New Retirement Plan)

- More Americans started their own businesses in 2009 and 2010 than at any other time in the past 15 years, according to the Kauffman Foundation's Index of Entrepreneurial Activity

- In 2010, 0.34 percent of Americans started their own business every month. Latinos and Asians experienced the most rapid growth in entrepreneurial activity, while the percentage of whites and blacks fell during the period. Rates rose for men, fell for women. Overall, start-up activity growth was highest among people aged 35 to 44. (Kauffman Foundation's Index of Entrepreneurial Activity)

- The number of new establishments for the year ending in March 2010 was lower than any year since the Bureau of Labor Statistics began collecting the data in 1994. Jobs created by start-ups sank to just under 2.5 million in 2010, down from a peak of 4.7 million in 1999. (U.S. News & World Report)

---

of that opportunity came by way of far-sighted men and women who could envision how an acre of cotton could give birth to a factory for spinning thread or how a burger joint that operated like a factory could revolutionize, for better or worse, the way America eats. Our discontent with the status quo and our dogged determination make us winners.

This uniquely American adventurer has a significant enemy to conquer in the 21st Century: the broken economy.

But first, we must address our own brokenness.

While everyone suffered in the epic economic turmoil that overtook us

---

Lifeblood Plus

A Great Enterprise is a financially healthy business committed to continuous improvement and guided by values and principles, led by an owner with a sense of purpose, perpetuity and legacy.

---

in 2008, business owners experienced a double-whammy. The impact of that double-whammy has made it hard to live into our role as innovators and pioneers and drivers of the economic machine.

The one-two punch looked like this:

One: No margin for missteps. Our margins are being squeezed from every direction—customers and clients, vendors, overhead, the rise in contracts based on competitive bids instead of long-term relationships or quality/service. There's no room in business, or in our lives, for failure.

Two: Capital has contracted. Banks aren't lending like they did. In fact, they're calling our loans and refusing to extend lines of credit and telling us our assets have no economic value. Capitalists seem to want too much for too little risk—they want a sure-thing combined with innovation that has enough wow-power to deliver a big return, and deliver it fast.

Either one of those factors, a decade ago, could have delivered the death-blow to an enterprise. Today, owners must figure out how to overcome both.

As a result, owners are fatigued like never before and experiencing something very similar to post-traumatic stress—all while being looked to for the heroic action that will set the economic landscape right again. We're expected to be the 21st Century pioneers and revolutionaries with the will and the creativity to redefine our economy. The world looks to us as leaders who can turn today's economic fail into an Entrepreneurial Revolution, securing our own future and the financial future of our society, as well.

The Owner's Voice

"With great change comes a responsibility to redefine yourself. I didn't realize this until I lived it. These are exciting times for us. Sure they may be a little uncertain but with that comes life and now you know you still have a pulse."

Hey, we're business owners. We do the impossible every day.

My prediction: We're up to this challenge. If anybody is, we are.

But it's going to require us to think differently, to redefine our success metrics and to reframe our dreams and our vision for the future.

The wise old foxes of my generation and the new generation of revolutionaries who have begun to emerge in the last decade are now in a position to collaborate on creating the economic and social direction of our world. ***This entrepreneurial revolution has the potential to exercise the single most powerful impact on how we live, work, learn and lead in this century and beyond.***

But that won't happen until we embrace a success model that's no longer based on the idea that we're business moguls in the corporate mold, building financial empires by acquiring more. *We must let go of that model and get back to the fundamentals.*

Revolutionary times

Here in the U.S., the role of private enterprise has long been to innovate, to create jobs, to boost the economic health of our communities—and I would add, especially in these times, to keep the entrepreneurial spirit going.

It's happened before, early in the last century. Although the 20th Century has been seen as the era of Corporate America, enterprising

Americans originally set the stage for the unprecedented economic and technological boom that shaped the world of the 20th Century. Enterprising Americans birthed the original ideas behind those corporations, back when they had a purpose greater than making stockholders wealthy—like changing the way people travel, communicate and experience life.

I was reminded of that in 1993, when I had just sold a successful business venture. I'd owned the company for eight years; a few smart (and lucky) moves had allowed me to realize a life-freeing profit.

I wasn't ready to retire, but I wasn't sure how to best steward the resources I'd just deposited in the bank. I had an idea I wanted to pursue, but I wanted to be sure it was the right way to invest my time and money.

To reach the right decision, I left for a solitary mountaintop retreat at Lake Lure, North Carolina, to spend time in self-evaluation and reflection. In the library at the Chalet Club, where I stayed, an autographed book lying on a table caught my eye.

Among Friends by James Newton was about the author's friendships with a singular group of brilliant and enterprising thinkers and doers who ignited great change during a time of deep societal and economic upheaval.

Lifeblood Plus

Professional Services Owners

Professionals—doctors, attorneys, architects, for example—with their own private practice may be Asset Builders, but their circumstances aren't quite like the solo business owner or the entrepreneur who has decided to build an enterprise.

A professional practice typically generates significant income, unlike other solo owners. By society's definitions, most professionals have been considered wealthy. But many of them live with the uneasy awareness that if they can no longer do the work—if they die or are disabled, either temporarily or permanently—the ride is over. The lifeblood dries up. Often, the enemy to sustainable wealth is the cost of lifestyle.

By using Asset Builder principles, professionals can position themselves to maintain their economic freedom by focusing on investments.

Thomas Edison, Henry Ford, Harvey Firestone, Charles Lindbergh, and a scientist and surgeon named Alexis Carrel are synonymous with the legacy of leadership and innovation that brought the U.S. to economic and political prominence in the 20th Century.

I was struck, as I read the book, by the parallels between their time and ours.

The first half of the 20th Century was a time of dramatic change. Our nation was in the midst of a classic paradigm shift that would revolutionize the way people lived. The simple act of putting people in automobiles changed their sense of time and space as profoundly as ours changed when we discovered that a click of the computer mouse could connect us to people around the world and provide us with information from every source imaginable. The automobile, of course, was only one of the astounding changes—there were also radio, motion pictures, telephone, flight, television.

Undergirded by the explosion in transportation and communication technology, these influential men made immeasurable contributions to our

---

Lifeblood Plus

Are you an Employee of your Business or an Asset Builder?

Score each statement on a 1-5 rating, with 1 being Strongly Disagree, 2 being Disagree, 3 being Undecided, 4 being Agree and 5 being Strongly Agree.

• When I make decisions about spending company resources, the priorities of the business come first, then family and estate planning priorities, then personal toys.

• My business is more of an investment than it is a personal expression for me.

• As the owner, I'm accountable to the leaders of my company regarding my compensation and the decisions I make about using company resources.

• Company leaders and key employees know their compensation structure assures financial rewards when they achieve specific goals that increase revenue or the equity value of the business.

---

nation's economy in the 20th Century.

This moment in time offers the same opportunity for entrepreneurs to write the story of the 21st Century and leave behind the legacy of another, equally profound economic and cultural revolution that will transform the way we live.

We start by getting back to the fundamentals, where we grow the value of our business asset by focusing on the value we offer.

Two faces of the Asset Builder [15]

Do you want to be part of an entrepreneurial revolution if it means focusing on something besides amassing piles of money?

If we feel tentative about the potential for an entrepreneurial revolution, the Chinese do not. When I visited China a few years ago, I learned

[15] In the first edition of *Lifeblood*, I used the term Wealth Builder, a type of business owner whose business asset was the centerpiece of a financial portfolio designed to achieve significant personal wealth. I am shifting the focus to building assets with value, a more relevant and timely focus during these times of rebuilding and recreating our economy.

• I openly share critical financial information with company leaders and key employees.

Here's what your total means:

1-5: An employee of your business, you still show some of the entitlement-mindedness of employees. Your decisions and your actions may threaten the health of your business.

6-10: Don't kid yourself. Your decisions may not appear to cause problems, but they will impact your long-term outcome.

11-15: It's Big Decision time: What do you really want from your business? Your inconsistency causes fear and uncertainty in your company.

16-20: Your instincts are good; you're likely a natural when it comes to wise decision-making around money. But you aren't yet living up to your tremendous wealth-building potential.

21-25: You have the mindset of a Business Asset Builder. Persevere in your journey.

---

that the government is engaged in social engineering to spawn entrepreneurship. So if we don't answer the call to revolutionize our economy with a new wave of entrepreneurship, the Chinese are ready to step into the breach.

Whether you see yourself as an owner with the desire and the potential to build an enterprise or as a one-gun slinger eager to make your contribution as a solopreneur or a mom-and-pop operating online, you can be an Asset Builder. And it is Asset Builders who will be the backbone of a successful and healthy economy for the 21st Century in America and around the world.

Although both are Asset Builders, I want to tell you about two different expressions of asset building. Both are valid. Both can contribute to economic health. And both are most likely to achieve their goals by operating out of the fundamentals.

One ownership style that is proving its staying power in these economic times is You, Inc. The other is the Owner CEO. They differ greatly in beliefs, strategies and objectives. Both can be economically sound. Both can satisfy their personal objectives while contributing to their communities. In other words, both can be Asset Builders —if they follow the fundamentals.

First, meet You, Inc.[16]

You, Inc.: Talent and trade-offs

The Internet has leveled the playing field and increased access to resources and information and prospective buyers for another breed of owners, sometimes called the solopreneur or You, Inc. This kind of micro-enterprise isn't new but it has proliferated since corporations cut loose hundreds of thousands of experienced, talented and motivated people, some with a severance package capable of capitalizing a start-up. I see recent college grads and other millennials, who have lost faith in what they

---

[16] You, Inc., has been part of my vernacular for the past ten years. Today, hundreds of books and articles embrace the language. Its origins have been lost.

see as a failed system, turn enthusiastically to the self-sufficiency they see in entrepreneurship, often with little but determination and desire.

The You, Inc., owner may desire to grow a small business, or even an enterprise. Or You, Inc., may prefer setting up a home office and remaining completely independent and relatively self-sufficient. Some have set themselves up as consultants, based on their industry experience pre-downturn. Some may be playing to a particular interest or skill set. The faces of You, Inc., are as broad as individual interests, talents and personal traits.

The Owner's Voice

"I have been an independent entrepreneur for 40 years, and could not discount the rewards of independence in the pursuit of my own business."

The successful You, Inc., may create software or design book covers or serve as a contract CFO or manage commercial real estate or operate a boutique on Main Street or lead adventure tours all over the globe. A dry cleaner, a techy, a designer and seller of jewelry, a small-scale events planner, a beekeeper—the list of fields in which solo entrepreneurs can compete in today's global marketplace is long and it is growing. And we all know a Realtor or attorney or physician who founded a solo practice and ultimately attracted others who wanted to help build that practice. I know of more than one caterer who started in her own kitchen and now owns multiple restaurants with a loyal clientele. The chances for self-expression are limitless for the You, Inc., with passion and initiative and focus.

The You, Inc., today could be an executive who was downsized out of his corporate position, a Millennial whose college exit led to an employment dead-end, an artist or other creator who embraced the lack of jobs as a chance for self-expression, a Boomer whose retirement crashed and burned in 2008 or a classic, entrepreneurial one-gun slinger who has seized this opportunity to strike out on her own.

Equally significant, the spirit of You, Inc., is found deep within *every* business owner, even those who have graduated to the level of enterprise builder. In these times, the most successful owners will be called to adapt and reinvent—a process that may force us to restore the You, Inc., at our core.

All the fundamentals and practices found in this book work just as effectively for You, Inc., as they do for an enterprise with 10 employees or 50 or 200.

The Owner's Voice

"Love a challenging market. The quick and the smart survive."

You, Inc., like any other business, is a living organism that will progress through life stages. As a result, many who fall into the You, Inc., category, may over time architect a true enterprise. Others have certain characteristics that make them more successful and more satisfied remaining in the category of You, Inc. Some are creatives who enjoy executing their gift or talent and have figured out how to turn that into economics. Some are classic introverts who have figured out how to plug into a niche in the marketplace without the stressors of a workplace community that cuts into their productivity or creativity or forces them into roles they aren't cut out for—managing others or hiring or building scalable systems, for example.

Fundamental beliefs of You, Inc., may include:

- My business is an expression of my gifts, my purpose or my calling.

- The business belongs to me and I call my own shots.

- My individualism/autonomy is worth more than significant economics.

- The business provides me with the freedom to travel or spend time with family or pursue some other passion.

- The business is a place where I can do what I do best without the distractions of organizational mechanics, routines or administration.

- My legacy will be found in the people I touch with my work.

The time is ripe for becoming a successful You, Inc.

The You, Inc., choice does come with trade-offs. Such small businesses almost always start out and remain solely dependent on the owner.

Earning potential more easily hits a ceiling. The market value of the company is compromised because no one will buy or invest in a company that relies on one person to run the money machine.

The Owner's Voice

"We're out-serving the competition and gaining customers.

Ultimately, You, Inc., must be content with its individual contribution, a smaller footprint and more limited economics than most enterprise builders hope to create.

Taken to an extreme, the You, Inc., belief system can lead to weak economics, isolation from the marketplace, and the kind of organizational chaos that threatens productivity, margins and profitability.

But the You, Inc., who knows, understands and operates within the fundamentals can be profitable, productive, extremely good at delivering a particular service or product, and deeply integrated into the lives of clients and customers.

You, Inc., can build an asset. An asset with less reach, less impact, less economic potential, frequently with less apparent legacy value. But an asset nevertheless. You, Inc., *can* be a real contributor to the economy and a legitimate Asset Builder. And who knows when You, Inc., will become the next Facebook.

The Owner CEO

The Owner CEO is an entirely different breed from You, Inc. Owner CEOs start out thinking in terms of growing a business by the more traditional model. They may be driven by a passion for a product or service, but they also have a strong desire is to build a legacy that survives them, can run without them (and thus has the potential for passive income) and is carried on into the next generation.

This breed of business owner, like You, Inc., also sees the need to control the environment in which she expresses her passion and purpose, but envisions an environment based on systems and procedures. Like any entrepreneur, the Owner CEO doesn't like being personally constrained by organizational mechanics, routines or administration, either, but understands the value of organizational architecture in creating a product or service that is scalable and duplicatable.

The Owner CEO and You, Inc., may be equally opportunity-minded, but the Owner CEO has equipped the business to respond to bigger opportunities by providing more resources of time, talent and money.

The Owner CEO typically inspires others with a grand vision for where the business is headed and what role each person plays in achieving that vision.

Fundamental beliefs of the Owner CEO may include:

- The business belongs to me and I call my own shots, although I know I'll need to cultivate leaders and outside advisors as the business grows.

- I'm willing to make personal sacrifices in the early days to invest in the future of this business.

- If I take care of the business, it will provide me with economic freedom.

- This business will be my legacy to the next generation.

Some of these beliefs have been challenged by the shift in our economy. Many owners who were strongly committed to growing a business feel betrayed not only by the "rules" they tried to follow but also by the American Dream itself. As their economics increased, they might have invested in real estate because it was a sure thing. Or they might have expanded into new territory, bought the latest and greatest equipment, adopted cutting edge technology, hired more people—all the earmarks of success that the business world believed in. In many cases, they feel these choices have failed them.

So one of the big challenges for the Owner CEO in today's economy is to figure out the new metrics for defining success—and get back to the fundamentals.

Building an asset

What You, Inc., and the Owner CEO can have in common is the choice to be Asset Builders, a choice that must be accompanied by the awareness that the playing field has changed, the rules of the game have changed, even the criteria for claiming a win have changed.

So what characteristics will mark the Business Asset Builder of the 21st Century?

First, Asset Builders view themselves as overseers or stewards of the asset and its resources of time, money and talent/people. They make choices and decisions based on their unique contribution value, designed to increase an asset's value to its customers, its vendors, its owner and its community.

Lifeblood Plus

Profile of Asset Builders

Asset Builders:

- Recognize that the business is the wealth-generating machine behind their financial portfolio
- Measure the success of the business based on earnings, net worth and potential for passive income generation
- Manage the finances of the business with an eye on the exit value
- Manage debt carefully
- Live comfortably, not extravagantly
- Earn the right to grow
- Measure use of resources against ROI
- Firewall personal & business finances
- Know how to multiply money, not bury it or consume it
- Maintain low debt-to-equity ratio
- Reinvest portion of profits to grow business
- Protect cash as the lifeblood of the business

As stewards, they are willing, as owners, to defer financial rewards in order to give the business a chance to recover or to finds its legs because they take the long view.

Because of that, today's Asset Builders will live comfortably but not lavishly. Their personal lifestyle and their business style will be lean. They will strive to find balance because they've realized, in the wreckage of these economic times, what's really valuable—family, faith, communities, serving a greater purpose in life, rather than growing the bank account.

At all times, fundamentals dictate the creation of cash flow and liquidity as well as the prudent stewardship of lifeblood resources. In lean times, nimbleness and adaptability are survival skills. And in times of economic stability, Asset Builders reinvest profit strategically to grow their business.

Asset Builders, in today's economy, will define growth and success in terms of the value they create for customers and clients and their ability to deliver that value to the marketplace in a way that allows for a degree of profit and sustainability.

This adjustment in expectations around success metrics is the mark of the Asset Builders' ability to trade on the promise and potential of tomorrow to weather challenges and make smart choices today. That ability is rooted in hope and in our vision of the future—two components of successful ownership that may be in even shorter supply than capital in today's economy.

Ownership Perspective

1. Have you chosen to make it a priority to pursue a lifestyle objective or an enterprise legacy through your business?

2. How could you see the face of America's economy changing if we experienced an upsurge in the health and adaptability of private enterprise? What implications might this have for your personal wealth objectives? For the hopes and dreams of business ownership in America?

3. What is your view on harvesting the rewards of your business versus investing in it as an asset?

The Asset Builder Code

*The vision of building a meaningful legacy
inspires people to unlock
the potential value of an enterprise.*

CHAPTER THREE
YOUR VISION, YOUR MONEY

"When the plow gets heavy, it takes a vision of something greater than money
to inspire others to pull the plow."

Times of great change present tremendous opportunity for building significant value, even if that value comes in a form we've never imagined. Wherever there is great pain, there is the opportunity for significant value.

Sadly, many of us will squander that opportunity because we've shut down our willingness to dream. That's a normal reaction to deep disappointment, loss and humiliation—things many of us have felt to some degree since the economic upheaval that began in 2008.

We're afraid to believe in ourselves, in our ability to beat this thing that has beaten so many of us. We've seen our dreams burned to ashes and we're exhausted by the effort to hold things together.

But now is not the time to cower away. As business owners, we know that. It will be what marks us as different.

Whenever there is trauma, people seek something to believe in. As entrepreneurs, we're probably accustomed to people looking to us for something to believe in. We are traditionally visionaries; one of our gifts is the ability to inspire others, to rally others behind an idea. But we're weary *and* wary of thinking about building something that has life beyond us. We feel betrayed by our dreams. But there is never a time to not dream. Ask Viktor Frankel.

Frankel was a Jewish neurologist and psychiatrist. He was also a Holocaust survivor who described in several books his strategy for concentration camp survival: to find meaning in even the harshest circumstances, meaning which then became his reason to keep going. This ability to hope and dream was the differentiator, for some, between living and dying.

Most of us, like Frankel, have identified something deep in our core that has kept us going through hard times.

Turning points

What did you experience in the final months of 2008? Shock? Denial? Loss? Discouragement? Fear? Most of us, whether we were business owners at the time or not, experienced some combination of those strong reactions. I know I did.

But I also experienced one of the most profoundly inspiring times of my life.

After gathering with the men of my church to process the fall-out from the meltdown, I felt called to communicate a message of hope to those men and to the owners and leaders in my network. So with no clear idea what would happen, I committed to delivering an electronic message to those people every day for the final 40 days of the year.

Those 40 messages became my fourth book, *40 Profound Concepts that Will Inspire Your Business Journey.*

Those 40 reflections also marked a turning point in my life. Spending those days in the arduous work of listening for inspiration, fresh insights, provoking wisdom and—yes—hope renewed my commitment to my deepest purpose in life. Those days strengthened my conviction that I am called to speak to and for business owners in this revolutionary time. It is that conviction that my work has meaning and purpose that has helped me sustain.

We must all believe in something bigger than us, bigger than mere survival, bigger certainly than the size of the payday at the end of the game. It is in that vision of something great where we'll find our most significant asset. The courage to dream will be the differentiator from those who are recovering, discovering and rebuilding sustaining business assets.

Vision is the wellspring for hope. And in difficult times, hope is the most fertile field for success.

Dusting off the dream

Most owners start with a vision. Some are great at making their vision inspiring for others – for leaders, employees, bankers, customers, family members. Some have learned to connect their vision with concrete goals and action plans and metrics that keep them focused and making progress. Some can hang onto their vision even in the bleakest of circumstances.

And a lot of us are learning how to dream again or recast our vision or downsize our aspirations.

The Owner's Voice

"My company's mission is greater than my needs."

In recent weeks I met with a talented young entrepreneur who founded a marketing agency a half dozen years ago. Like many in his field, he discovered that marketing dollars were among the first cut from the budget as businesses have adapted. The decline in client base and revenue forced him to rethink his business model. But he did more than look at margins and overhead and service model. He went all the way back to his You, Inc., the original passion that inspired his initial vision for his agency.

Today, he has reshaped his business model to serve a unique niche—emerging brands with the potential to overtake the big brands in their industry.

Over the years, one of my favorite pieces of work with business owners is to help them mine their dreams for a vision that can be 1) tied to concrete goals and metrics; 2) is an expression of their companies' unique brilliance; and 3) reminds everyone in an organization how they contribute to achieving the vision. The resulting Vision Map becomes the roadmap to the future, giving shape to strategic planning and decision-making.

Vision Mapping takes owners to the core of what motivates them and what matters to them. It is where they find their purpose and their significance, the thing that gets them up even on mornings when the weight of business ownership feels overwhelming.

One young enterprise builder who comes to mind owned a disaster relief company. He and his crew get called in after hurricanes and floods and other events that most of us would be just as happy to avoid. But this owner and his crew wade in, for weeks and months at a time.

Sometimes, when this owner watched his team working in the rubble of a natural disaster, he glimpsed something else. He could almost see the day when the first name to come to mind for a homeowner or insurance adjustor following a catastrophe would be his company. He

---

Lifeblood Plus

Mapping Your Vision

Vision can be limited if we define or describe it without exploring our dreams. So creating Vision begins by igniting the thinking process. Here are the guidelines for touching off your imagination:

Identify Core Values: Defining Vision begins with passion for an idea, as well as a deep sense of purpose. What are you striving to achieve? What are the beliefs and core values that drive you? Look for the key words that resonate.

See the Future: Translate the beliefs, the values, the excitement, the purpose into changes, actions, results at some point over the horizon. Allow the beliefs to take shape. Think symbolically about beliefs, values, goals.

Commit it to Paper: Write it down. Create symbols. Draw pictures. Refine it. Shape and sharpen the idea. Make it both concrete—*the company will have four distinct divisions*—and abstract—*customers will value our commitment to their needs.*

Articulate it to Others: Take the Vision to others, express it with all the power and passion you have. Tell them how you will move from the present to the future, and bring them with you.

could envision a network of franchises dispatching trucks with his company's logo on the door.

As I worked with this owner, he acknowledged that few people in his organization knew the full story of his vision. "It was like a whisper chain," he said, "where the end message is nothing like the beginning."

We helped this owner give expression to his vision and he was well on his way to turning it into reality. Then along came a disaster his company wasn't equipped to clean up—an economic disaster that created wreckage across the marketplace.

Today, this owner has picked through the rubble like everyone else. He's still here and my prediction is that he'll come through this stronger than ever as he practices the fundamentals we'll talk about in Part Two of the book.

He, like the rest of us, must be able to dust off the dream and use it to propel him forward.

Starting with the remnant

There will always be times when we're too bewildered or exhausted or discouraged to think about vision. If we do think about it after major setbacks, we can be too angry or humiliated or gun-shy to even want to go there.

I've never seen a time when it was more challenging for people to believe in a vision that reaches beyond the next bend in the road. We've been burned and we don't want to be burned again. This is true for owners and their leaders and their families and their bankers and their vendors and their customers.

Even *Time* magazine, on its July 2, 2012, cover, posed this question about the American Dream: Is It Still Real?

An HBO series in the summer of 2012 grabbed viewers with a four-minute opening rant that argued this position: *The U.S. is no longer the greatest country in the world.* Facebook and Twitter talked about it; so did other newscasters like the character in the show. The video clip, I believe, went viral. Why? Because too many of us, deep in our hearts, had that same fear.

More importantly, though, I believe the program and the clip caught fire because so many of us wanted the dream restored. That begins, at least in part, with our willingness as business owners to reconstruct a viable vision for our businesses.

We do that by starting with a remnant of purpose from the core of our being.

Seizing the remnant

Every business has that core, unless it was built on the wrong values, the wrong purpose in the first place.

Where do we look for our core? I suggest, even for those who are still operating a business of substantial size, that we go all the way back to the vision for our personal You, Inc.

That's where every owner must start. Even second- or third-generation business owners must dig deep into their own core to find out if there's an entrepreneurial spirit there. If not, the successful transfer from one generation to the next will be elusive.

Start with these questions:

- What is at my core?
- What passion or purpose drives me?
- What can't be taken away from me?
- What did my dreams of the future look like before the market-place crashed?
- When do I feel most alive? When can I still feel a spark?
- What beliefs and values are at the foundation of my dreams?
- What do I want to be remembered for?
- What is the legacy only I can create?

Somewhere in the answer to those questions is the remnant with which you begin to dream again and build vision again and entertain hope for the future again. When you seize that remnant, your hope for the future begins to revive and gain strength.

Reclaiming my core

For the last dozen years, I've operated multiple companies under one corporate umbrella. One is a consulting firm that works with business owners and their leaders to build healthy enterprises. One represents owners who want to sell their companies or find capital. The third company, the Institute for Business Owners, develops and owns and licenses the use of my intellectual capital—my writings, the Enterprise Builder System, tools and materials for business owners, one-on-one owner coaching, content for retreats and more.

The Owner's Voice

"I dream of the day when I become inspired again."

Almost ten years ago, when only two of those business entities existed, my little corporation was at a crossroad. We could build out the consulting firm or we could build out the Institute, but we didn't have the resources of time, money and people to build out both at once. At that point, my partners and I were smart enough to take our own advice—we brought in some outside advisors to give us more objective input about which business to focus on.

All three of the consulting firms we brought in told us that the Institute was our greatest differentiator in the market and that it was also poised to be the most significant source of revenue with e-commerce about to explode.

We didn't listen. Or maybe we just didn't believe.

At that point, our primary source of revenue was the consulting firm and not the Institute. Entrepreneurship flourished in the marketplace and, with it, the need for owners to receive advisory services on healthy growth strategies. We made an intentional decision not to make the riskier move to funnel resources into the Institute and gamble that the internet would become a powerful platform for monetizing intellectual capital.

We focused on the consulting company and allowed the Institute to continue to do what it did, quietly and on the sidelines.

We made that choice based on economics, despite the fact that the Institute reflected my deepest purpose. It always had been and it continued to be as we built the consulting firm over the next decade.

The Owner's Voice

"There is nothing better than having control of your future and your earning ability."

Then came the great recession. Immediately, my companies adapted. As I expected, the market for consultants to owners of small businesses lost some momentum. Finally, in 2012, came the Black Thursday I wrote about in chapter one, when the collapse of a major deal forced additional adaptation for my three companies. It was painful at first. Then it came to me: This rocky patch created the opportunity for me to build an electronic platform for serving owners in exactly the way that everyone envisioned a dozen years before.

The downturn has given me the chance to dig deeper into my true purpose while expanding my reach in the marketplace, a growth move that now excites me every morning when I get up.

Also, since the materials we use with our consulting practice have gone digital, which enables us to empower more people with our tools.

We are among the survivors of this economic upheaval because we, like our clients, can be stomped on but not killed. And the vision that is sustaining me right now is a remnant of that core no one can take away from me.

Unlocking the potential

If you're a business owner, whether an Owner CEO or a You, Inc., you have a vision. We all do. If we didn't, we'd be pushing a mouse for somebody else, checking off the days till payday. Vision serves many purposes in a business.

- It inspires people to follow us.

- It helps us survive challenging times.

- It gives focus to our decision making.

Here's the most important purpose vision serves: ***Vision inspires people—that includes us—to unlock the potential value of our companies.***

A clearly articulated vision drives the business toward accomplishments that are loftier than economic gain. This is actually the foundation on which economic gain rests. Vision gives people an itinerary and a roadmap for the destination they're striving toward.

Here's an example of what I mean. A friend in my community who owns a service business has had a hard time sustaining success. She struggles along, then nails a big contract and thinks she's arrived at a sustainable pinnacle. She doesn't consistently attract high talent and when she does land talented players, she can't hang onto them. The pipeline doesn't deliver another big contract in a timely fashion, the boom goes bust and she struggles again until she nails the next big contract. Sometimes, when the boom was big enough, she added to her facility and her staff and all the markers of significant success. But when the recession hit, she was in way over her head. The business folded.

Now, there were no doubt a number of reasons my friend couldn't make the business cross the chasm to build an economically sustainable enterprise. She built her vision before earning the right, for starters. But there's another one worth mentioning: She never communicated a significant vision to her organization, so her employees filled in the blanks for her. From their perspective, the owner's vision went something like this: "If you all work hard, one day *I'll* own a home in the mountains."

Guess what? Nobody goes the extra mile for that.

I know my friend had a greater vision. But she never recognized the significance of that vision in driving the asset-building engine.

How does vision unlock the potential value of a business? It's not really possible to reduce this to a linear process, but the pathway looks something like this:

Vision > Belief > Commitment > Priorities >

Choices > Habits & Disciplines > Results

Vision enables others to see goals and accomplishments that are worth working hard to achieve—worth sacrifice, even. When people see and **believe** in the vision, they are willing to make a **commitment** to do what is needed to make the vision a reality. Once people have committed to achieving certain goals, identifying the right **priorities** becomes more clear. And focusing on those priorities gives clarity and decisiveness to the **choices** that become the consistent **habits and disciplines** that drive the right **results**.

One of those results may be economic gain.

The success literature of the past told us this pathway was a sure thing. We know that was a myth then and it's still a myth. But it's not a myth that it takes something greater than money to inspire us and others to pull the plow, especially when pulling the plow gets hard. Some of us just haven't given much thought to what our vision is. We haven't dug deep to get past the obvious—*I want to make a lot of money*—to the substantive, like making a difference in the world or improving life conditions for others or doing something better than it's ever been done. There's nothing wrong with making a lot of money as an owner. That can be a good metric; businesses need to make more money. But that can't be all there is to your vision.

Every day we make dozens of decisions that impact the vision, our ability to achieve it and, thus, the lifeblood of the business.

When we know our vision, we'll know the pathway to follow to achieve our ownership objectives. We'll know whether we want to be an Asset Builder. Then we will be strongly positioned and highly motivated to play the game by the Smart Money Fundamentals.

Ownership Perspective

1. Do you believe there is an inextricable link between enterprise wealth and the owner's clarity about vision?

2. Do you have a compelling vision that sets the stage for enterprise wealth? If not, why not?

3. Do the leaders in your business understand your vision?

PART TWO

FUNDAMENTALS

The Seven Smart Money Rules

1. Learn to Earn

2. Eyes on the Money

3. Make Cash Flow

4. Avoid the Debt Sinkhole

5. Hedge Your Bets

6. Leverage Down

7. Think Like a Capitalist

CHAPTER FOUR
SMART MONEY RULES

*"The owners with the greatest likelihood of success
weren't using some mysterious silver bullet;
they had adopted a complete shift in mindset."*

Because of my work and because of my passion for entrepreneurship, I spend my days shoulder-to-shoulder, toe-to-toe with women and men who are in the trenches of this epic entrepreneurial revolution. I see their points of brilliance and I see their minor misfires and their colossal screw-ups. They tell me the secrets even their spouses don't know, much less the other business owners in their circle of friends and colleagues.

As I walk with them on their journey, I've always found myself wondering about the difference between the owners who are making it and the ones who aren't. Their walk and their talk don't seem so very different. But the winners at the enterprise game must know a secret. They must've cracked some kind of secret code that separates the ones who never quite make it from the ones who make it really big.

These business owners—the one-gun slingers and the freedom seekers, the entrepreneurs who cross the chasm and the ones who hit the canyon floor—taught me the rules that allow the Asset Builder to succeed while the rest struggle. The rules that enable Asset Builders to adapt to change and make their assets better while others freeze in the headlights and die.

When the Great Recession began in 2008, I discovered something even more valuable: The owners with the greatest likelihood of success weren't using some mysterious silver bullet; they had adopted a complete mindset. A mindset so radical that it left them better equipped to survive a major economic disruption. I also discerned that the mindset was equally successful whether these owners were leading a mature enterprise, an emerging company or a You, Inc.

I call this mindset the Asset Builder's Code. At the center of that code are seven key concepts around money—the Smart Money Rules.

The seven Smart Money Rules that I've distilled from the experiences of Asset Builders are:

1. Learn to earn. Embedded in Asset Builders' consciousness is a keen sense of profit. If it doesn't make a profit, it isn't a business asset, it's a liability. If we want the business to serve our needs, we must first serve its needs by learning how to earn a profit. The key to profit is tied to four concepts covered in Chapter 4.

2. Eyes on the money. Asset Builders know the three measures of healthy finances and how to stay on top of them in about ten minutes a week. Master that discipline and gain clarity about the single most important tool for taking control of your enterprise in Chapter 5.

3. Make cash flow. We love revenue and we love profit. But Asset Builders' understanding of and respect for the link between money and time keep the doors open. Understand why and how to keep the cash flowing in Chapter 6.

4. Steer clear of the debt sinkhole. The lure of debt is a silent killer. Business owners often don't realize their financial health is endangered until it is too late to survive—a lesson that many learned too late to survive the downturn. Asset Builders understand: a) how easy it is to slip into debt and how hard it is to crawl out of debt; b) the difference between good debt and bad debt; c) how to develop a debt strategy; and

d) how to maintain the upper hand with your lenders. All are covered in Chapter 7.

5. Hedge your bets. Business is risky, but Asset Builders have an instinct for hedging against the odds and avoiding over-exposure in the risky decisions that must be made every day. Asset Builders keep their options open while narrowing their assumptions, a practice covered in Chapter 8.

6. Leverage down. Getting stuck in the entrepreneurial mindset of creation and innovation can block Asset Building. At certain life stages of the enterprise, we must create, we must hunt and we must innovate. Other stages ask us to elevate up and out of the organization, to regain perspective on the big picture and focus on the vision. At other stages, it is time go deep into our companies to tap sources of "capital" that are easily overlooked. In Chapter 9, learn how we can heighten the awareness of the gold right under our noses and leverage it to increase the value of our business asset.

7. Think like a capitalist. This final Smart Money Rule represents a significant stage in the life of an Asset Builder, and it has never been more important than it is in this time when banks have changed the rules of the game now and for the foreseeable future. We've had to accept the fact that bankers are not investing in our businesses in the way we once believed. The term relationship banker is the language of another era. We must own the responsibility for capitalizing the continuous adaptation that will be necessary to sustain in an uncertain and ever-changing marketplace. Chapter 10 explores thinking like a capitalist in order to achieve the true asset value and equity potential of a business.

Of course, playing by the Smart Money Rules isn't the end game for committed Asset Builders. The game is complex. But the first step in cracking the Asset Builder's Code is to play smart with company finances. From the basics, which are so fundamental that some of us fail to appreciate the complexities, to the practice of capital planning, a practice that few master and many stumble over, Smart Money Rules equip us to elevate our game.

Smart Money Rule #1:
Learn to Earn

Business value is not measured by revenue;
it is measured by what's left over at the end of the day.

CHAPTER FIVE
SMART MONEY RULE #1:
LEARN TO EARN

"Let me be the first to deliver the sad news.
No profit equals no business."

Want to know how successful you ***really*** are as a business owner? Look at it through the eyes of a capitalist.

Through that lens, here's the main question you'll want to answer: What's the return on investment?

Of course, a capitalist wants other answers, too. Is it a viable business model? Is there a consumer willing to shell out money for your product or service? Is it scalable? A capitalist isn't impressed that you're working yourself to death, putting in 60 to 80 hours a week, paying yourself below market value. In fact, the shrewd capitalist might see those dubious badges of honor as signs that you haven't learned the most basic lesson of ownership: how to earn a profit.

In any given year, I walk potential investors through a number of our client businesses. I vet the capitalists I work with as diligently as capitalists vet investment opportunities, to make sure they're interested in healthy enterprises that offer solid partnership potential, the chance to put their money to work making more money—for everyone involved.

The business most likely to attract capital in these lean times is one that is adapting its way into a healthier segment of its industry and exhibits the same characteristics of financial health that capitalists have always been interested in. One of my most trusted capitalists tells me that capital is most valuable when it is applied to move a business from one state of health to another.

The industry of the day will come and go, but the fundamental of

Lifeblood Plus

Myths about Profit

As savvy as we business owners are, our heads are often full of fantasy about the money of our business.

- We think the value of the business asset is measured by its top-line revenue.

- We think if we work hard the money will take care of itself.

- We think capital equipment equals a valuable business.

- We think a brilliant innovation delivers profit.

- We think having enough money to pay the Overhead Monster must surely mean we're profitable

The Asset Builder knows those are all false assumptions. And false assumptions will kill you.

earning power never goes away. Capitalists are not and never have been interested in the business that has not learned to earn. The first person they look to in order assess this fundamental is the owner: Does she know how to earn a dollar?

A few years into the recession I visited a client company with one of my most trusted capital sources. The owner of a regional business with a reputation for fast growth over more than a decade, my client had developed a concept for an eco-friendly product with appeal to larger companies with high use of certain non-renewable office supplies. This owner was on the precipice of a big move, but had no working capital to finance the adaptation.

So I brought in a capitalist to take a look at what appeared to be a strong candidate for investment. After several weeks of due diligence, this capitalist concluded that his hard-earned capital would not be funding this promising innovation. Why?

First he saw a product that could not deliver sufficient margins. He saw an offering to clients that would not easily scale. Most significantly, he saw an owner who did not fully understand that the business model had little hope of generating the kind of revenue necessary to fund the ongoing innovation the marketplace would demand. The need for R&D would be continuous and costly.

This was an owner who knew how to churn, but had not learned to earn.

What's left over?

The good venture capitalist understands the delicate economic balance in every business. This tricky balance is maintained by paying attention to a simple equation.

How much comes in?

How much goes out?

What's left over?

Lifeblood Plus

Seven-Minute Drill

I can tell in seven minutes whether an owner runs his business by the numbers by asking seven questions. Once upon a time I could ask these questions and find that owners had no idea how to answer them; today, owners who never learned to answer these questions aren't around any more.

1. Do you know the average revenue for the last three months?

2. Do you know the average profit for the last three months?

3. What do you project for the next three months?

4. How much money do you have in the bank?

5. What are the balances and aging of your accounts payable and your accounts receivable?

6. What is your monthly break-even?

7. Do you know the profit margin on every product/service you offer?

Too many of us measure our success solely on the answer to the first question. *How much comes in?* A hundred grand in sales revenue the first year? *Whew! Dodged the bullet.* A quarter million? *Good. We're hanging in there.* Two-point-five? *Great!* Twenty…no, *fifty* million? *The sky's the limit!*

But the Asset Builder has learned that paying attention only to the first question—how much comes in—won't keep a business afloat for long. In today's economy, we've all seen the enterprise that turned upside down in a heartbeat because in times that weren't so lean ownership equated churning revenue with being profitable.

The Owner's Voice

"Clients want things for less but with more deliverables. Employees want increases, but the revenue isn't growing. The ability to diversify is our only saving grace."

Failing to pay attention to the whole equation might not kill a business today or even next month. But revenue alone—even outstanding revenue—won't keep a business alive and healthy for the long haul. Because there will always be lean times. And in the lean times, those who only know how to churn have no experience in the hard realities of earning.

Remember, it's the lifeblood that keeps the business alive.

Lifeblood isn't solely about what comes into the business. It's also about what flows out of the business, and the timing of the flow in and out. The lifeblood must flow. Not clot. Not hemorrhage.

Flow.

Learning to earn means paying attention to all parts of the financial equation that ultimately add up to profit. One of the key measures of healthy lifeblood is profit. But too many business owners don't fully understand the complexities and the delicate balance that make up profit. Here's one way the Asset Builder measures profit:

Profit is the portion of revenue that is available for uses above and beyond the day-to-day needs of the business.

When you've written checks to pay for materials and supplies, what's left?

After you've paid the rent and the health insurance and the payroll, what's left?

When taxes have taken a bite, what's left?

When you're current with every monthly obligation, what's left?

What's that? There's nothing left, except maybe a little red ink?

Then let me be the first to deliver the sad news. No profit equals no business. In start-up, you may shoestring the operation for a time while you catch up with profitability. At key junctures, you may forego healthy profit to fund the right growth moves. In a recession like the one we've experienced in recent years, profit may ebb and flow, especially as a business invests to adapt to marketplace shifts. But over time, like a heart with blocked arteries, the business will starve from clogged cash flow. Every limb and organ of the business will deteriorate from lack of lifeblood.

Lifeblood Plus

The Laws of Great Enterprise

The first requirement for learning to earn is having a viable business model, which leads to a healthy economic formula. A robust business model follows certain laws that aren't optional. I think of them as the Laws of Great Enterprise. How does your business stack up?

1. The Law of Market Niche. Do you provide a product or service that is highly desirable to some clearly identifiable segment of the marketplace?

2. The Law of Unique Brilliance. Have you found your company's unique fingerprint in the market? Do you know how your company rises above others in the marketplace? Do you consistently operate out of that giftedness?

3. The Law of Customers. An enterprise is as healthy as its relationship with customers. Is your customer base healthy, balanced and loyal?

4. The Law of Profit. A business without a profit is not an asset—it is a liability. Do you demand to know the return on investment in every key use of time and money before you pull the trigger? Or do you fire and pray?

5. The Law of Optimization. Optimization is a fancy word for making the best use of resources to achieve the best possible results. Are your company's resources of money, time and talent applied strategically and effectively to achieve specific goals and outcomes?

Lifeblood Plus

Curbing Cash Loss

Cash-loss factors are different for every company. But if we pay attention to three specific strategies we can begin to impact our cash problems: 1) a capital strategy, 2) a pricing strategy and 3) a strategically-timed collections and payables strategy. For some types of businesses, a fourth category where significant cash is lost is inventory management.

Minimize the impact of growth with a capital strategy. Business owners still have the tendency to understate the impact of growth. More money, more customers, more products, more territory, more services—surely "more" will solve our problems. But growth without sufficient margins to support the growth can put unexpected strain on resources. Overhead goes up, the need for equipment or inventory goes up, mistakes come with a higher price tag. Growth can gobble up cash.

Minimize the potential impact of high service, low margins with a pricing strategy. Today's market conditions seem to demand that we ignore the fundamental correlation between our profit margins and the level of service we can afford to give our clients and customers. We struggle with the realities of a marketplace that buys on price but expects concierge service as part of the package. A faulty pricing strategy can keep margins so low that it's impossible to develop a profitable business.

Minimize the impact of an anemic balance sheet with a focused collections and payables strategy. Here's a critical intersection of time and money. When money comes in slowly and goes out rapidly, it creates a cash crunch. When we allow accounts receivable to extend one day beyond industry standards, we open the door for our customers to erode our cash flow. We're letting our customers use our money interest-free. We may also operate with a hair-trigger payables policy—it's not due until the 15th, but we write our checks on the 1st; if so, we're letting our vendors use our money interest-free. We're choosing to be a cash flow victim. The answer is to negotiate the best terms on both ends, manage collections so that we get our money on time and never pay our vendors a day earlier than terms require.

Minimize the cash tied up in unproductive inventory. This is another area where the relationship between time and money is apparent. The goods sitting in your warehouses are unproductive; you can't bill for them so they are costing you money. The longer they sit there, the more they cost you. Libraries have been written about inventory control. But simply stated, get it in and out the door as quickly as your industry allows.

Without profit to support positive cash flow, you don't have a business, you have a potentially dangerous liability.

Maybe you have an enjoyable entrepreneurial pursuit. Or a hobby. At worst, you have a liability. No profit, no business. And without a viable business, of course, nobody's building sustainable economic health. And if we're not building economic health, we're just another employee with the glorified title of Owner.

Taking care of business

If we want the business to serve our needs, we must first serve its needs by learning what it takes to earn a profit. Learning to earn can be boiled down to mastering three key focal points:

1. Knowing the numbers.

2. Selling it right.

3. Managing costs.

Suddenly, business ownership is slightly more complicated than just finding somebody who'll pay us to do what we love and cashing the check. Playing by Smart Money Rules—the only game that pays off in building ongoing, stable economics—demands mastering those three focal points.

1. Know the numbers. Maybe you have all the numbers at your fingertips, or in your head. You know the sales figures from last month or even last year. You know the big-ticket items that make up the bulk of your overhead. But how many of *these* numbers do you know:

- What's your break-even in sales revenue?

- What are your fixed costs?

- What is your gross profit percentage?

- If you sell different lines of goods or services, what is the gross profit margin for each?

- What kind of revenue can you realistically expect given the dynamics of your industry or niche?

57

- What are the total cash obligations you must pay each week or each month, including the nickels and dimes that soon add up to hundreds and thousands?

Gaining a comprehensive picture tells us 1) what kind of numbers are probable within our industry; 2) what kind of numbers we require to fulfill the basic needs of the business; 3) what our ideal economic formula looks like; and 4) how our actual performance stacks up against what's probable and what's required.

Does the reality of our particular niche in our particular industry allow for healthy economics? If so, by making sure we know our numbers daily, weekly, monthly, we can then calculate and recalculate the numbers over time in order to move in the direction of our ideal formula.

So whether we are striving to reach profitability for the first time or working to elevate to the level of profitability that allows for sustainable economic health, knowing the numbers is the most basic requirement for achieving profitability.

Lifeblood Plus

Selling It Right

Selling it right isn't one decision. It's a series of decisions that will ultimately help us achieve the right product or service, the right price and the right customers. To get the right answers, ask the right questions at every step.

1. Is the product or service priced to match the risk threshold of this customer?

2. Can I afford to take this opportunity with these margins? Will these margins allow me to make my client/customer more valuable and, thus, prove my own value?

3. Are we cultivating the customers/clients who are likely to be with us for the long haul?

4. Are we willing to work outside our sweet spot in order to close the deal?

5. Does this customer consistently deplete our time or energy with demands that are above and beyond the parameters of our terms? Is

Knowing our numbers means ***understanding what the numbers are telling us.*** If we haven't studied all those numbers and plugged them into an equation that shows us where the business really stands, we don't know the numbers. We're just playing with them. Until we understand the numbers, we don't know what conditions we need in order to serve our clients *and* make a profit. We have to know the numbers.

2. Sell it right. Maximizing revenue potential is a first step in achieving the numbers in our ideal economic formula. Getting to the right numbers on the sales side of the equation entails:

- Selling the ***right product or service***

- Selling at the ***right price point*** to achieve the ***right profit margins*** to achieve a healthy balance between volume and profit

- Selling to the ***right customers*** under the ***right terms*** and conditions to improve cash flow and/or minimize working capital needs

that because customer terms are too vague or unstated? Have we failed to create conditions for success?

6. Can we create the efficiencies of scale that are necessary for healthy profit margin with this product/service and these relationship terms?

7. What will we trade off if we choose to step outside our area of giftedness, or serve the customer who diverts us, or live with margins that starve the business? Will the price be market share? Standards of quality? Efficiencies? Will the failure to focus mean we don't get quite as good as we could be?

8. Can we live with these trade-offs for a season in order to bridge the gap to the next stage of healthy growth?

9. If these compromises become our company's *modus operandi,* is it possible that the business fails to gel or reach full potential?

10. How likely are we to build business wealth if we make these trade-offs beyond the short-term? Central to our return to fundamentals in the downturn has been focus: knowing who we're best at serving and doing what we do best.

Right product, right price point, right customers—it's a balancing act. Too often we make some of these decisions by default or by focusing on one element—the price we want, for example—and not all three.

Sometimes it's easy to see the effects of faulty pricing strategy, but hard to trace the effects back to the root problem.

A local landscaping company was in high-growth mode a few years ago, before the real estate market collapsed. Word was spreading that Andy's crew served the production home builder better than anyone else. He was signing up business in the next county and the next state; business was hotter than hot. Every morning when his trucks hit the road, Andy saw dollar signs.

What he didn't realize was that he was watching those dollar signs wave goodbye on the way out the front gate.

Lifeblood Plus

A Capitalist Looks at Earning Power

I've done my due diligence with capitalists to understand what's on their minds and what they're looking for in an investment opportunity in these uncertain times. Here's what they're telling me:

Fundamentals rule. Are you liquid? Is the balance sheet healthy? How's your debt situation? Has the Overhead Monster been caged? Are the wheels falling off the business model? Are margins predictable?

Vision is out, survival and adaptability are in. Capitalists measure performance in survivability. No high-risk start-ups, no turnarounds. Can you demonstrate reasonable profit and stability over the last three to five years? Do you know how to land on your feet when you're flipped?

Fluidity beats innovation. Capitalists aren't bold enough to speculate on the cutting edge. Don't lead with your big idea. They want proof you know how to execute and create liquid profit to pay the bills. Then they will believe you can create a winning big idea. Capitalists love big ideas, but they believe them when they see you can execute and not run out of cash.

Think exit. Capitalists want to put their money at play, hit it over the fence (or at least know where the fence is), cash out and get off the field in a hurry. No capitalist wants to get their money stuck in your business. The capitalist wants money in motion.

The business kept rolling in but every month the books looked a little more anemic. How could the company be doing more business and making less money? It just didn't add up. Andy's frustration grew. Was the bookkeeper miscalculating? Was somebody stealing from him?

Well, yes. In fact, Andy was stealing from himself every time he signed a contract.

"I finally realized we were still pricing the jobs like we did when they were five miles away," Andy said. "Revenue was up, but travel costs were killing us." Not just once, but job after job; this kind of cost creep is common—and commonly overlooked—during times of transition.

The Owner's Voice

"A lot of people...are financial nitwits. You have to be conservative, control your expenses...too many entrepreneurs believe in entitlements, which kills profit faster than anything."

Developing a pricing strategy means understanding all the factors that impact the cost of delivering the product or service, then paying attention to those factors.

3. Manage costs. Most of us remember the days of the efficiency experts. They were seen as the solution to managing costs by finding ways for us to yield the same results for fewer dollars. There was good value in that, and there still is. But in today's world, containing costs requires the discipline of prudent decision-making linked to a thorough knowledge of our economic equation (knowing our numbers).

High on my weekly work plan is containing the cost of goods, the cost of sales and the expenses of overhead. At every turn, we need to know: How much is this going to cost? Are there hidden costs that will come back to haunt us? Raw goods, labor, transportation, equipment, administration, supplies, facility—dollars spent in every area potentially represent dollars we could've saved.

It all starts with a detailed budget. This isn't a lesson in budgeting; we can all find plenty of sources to help with that. But we need to remember that Asset Builders are rigorous and disciplined in their budgeting practices.

Here's what the budget does for us: enables us to track expenses every month and compare those numbers to the numbers projected in the budget. If they're different— and they often are—we must understand why. Answering "why" pinpoints the problems and points toward the solutions.

I'm known in my business for scrutinizing every nickel we spend. I know that nickels add up to dollars and dollars add up to hundreds, which compound and build economic health. For every expense—that includes rent and payroll and marketing—I ask myself how it connects to revenue and whether it will deliver some kind of return. I keep overhead low. I link compensation to measurable performance. I walk the razor's edge of healthy profit margin, trying not to shortchange clients by giving too little or giving them Neiman Marcus service for Wal-Mart prices.

> ## The Owner's Voice
>
> *"We have had a chance to regroup and recover and be even more agile and flexible and watchful for the changing economy."*

Containing costs is certainly far more complicated than squeezing nickels. It requires vigilance and a willingness to be accountable for decisions around money. But do I squeeze nickels? You bet I do, whenever possible. Most importantly, I try to squeeze them where it makes the most sense.

We'll never make a fortune squeezing nickels; but if we don't squeeze them, we can lose it all.

Retained earnings

Learning to earn seems elementary. If we work hard, surely the money takes care of itself. Wrong.

Then surely we can count on our accountant or our bookkeeper— our CFO, for Pete's sake, look how much we're paying her!—to pay attention to the numbers. Wrong.

We're the owner. It's our job. Others may be diligent. But nobody else will ever care as much as us. No one else will ever have as much on the line as we do. If we've learned anything from the Great Recession, most of us have learned that.

At its most basic level, learning to earn means weighing every decision against its impact on the lifeblood of our business. For every dollar used to serve customers and keep the doors open, Asset Builders ask: Is it necessary? Is it enough? Is it too much?

Learning to earn isn't about being miserly. It's about **retained earnings**—earnings that aren't obligated to run the business, but can be shifted to the other side of the firewall, to be deployed at the right time. That money may be re-invested in the business or it could be used for other investments that can create wealth.

But if it's still tied up in the operation of the business, if it's still necessary to keep the business afloat, we haven't retained it and we haven't earned it. Business value is built on what is retained.

Ownership Perspective

1. Do you think "profit" all the time?

2. What would a smart capitalist say about the potential investment opportunity of your business? Should his answer have some impact on the way you, as a stockholder, look at your business?

3. Do you measure the success of your business by the earnings of the company or the size of your salary? Or do you measure the healthiness of your business on its adaptive strength? Is what you're doing preparing your business for its next life stage?

Smart Money Rules #2:

Eyes on the Money

*Never assume that anyone else
will pay attention to the money.
Only the owner has enough at stake
to be constantly vigilant.*

Chapter Six
Smart Money Rule #2:
Eyes on the Money

"Are your eyes on the money? If not, how can you be sure that you're making any?"

About 25 years ago, I was learning Smart Money Rules the hard way as the owner of a company with factories, warehouses, trucks and expensive capital equipment. We looked healthy. Orders were coming in, product was going out. We were beginning to come out of the nosedive the company had been in when I purchased it a few years earlier for the cost of a good used car.

Still, cash was hard to come by. So hard to come by that sometimes we just didn't have any. But it seemed to me that we were juggling the bills pretty successfully, figuring out the drop-dead dates for the ones that *had* to be paid and holding the ones that could wait until our customers paid us. Nobody seemed to be sending collection agencies after us, so I assumed I was playing the money game pretty cleverly.

One day while rushing down the highway to a customer appointment, I picked up my mobile phone to prep for the meeting with my VP. But when I dialed his number, I found myself talking to someone from the mobile phone company. I was confused and irritated by the distraction. The customer service rep said, "Our records indicate that you haven't paid your bill."

Insignificant details. I was on big stuff. I tried being reasonable. "I need to make this call."

"I understand," the person from customer services said, sounding equally reasonable. "But we need to get paid."

Now I was indignant. "There must be some mistake."

The only mistake, as it turned out, was my failure to keep my eyes on the money. I had no idea we were behind in our accounts payable, especially in lifeline services like utilities. If I'd been paying attention, I would never have been blindsided. The lifelines of the business would never have been starved of their lifeblood.

The Owner's Voice

"When I stop listening to the news and listen to the marketplace, revenues increase each month."

Where the buck stops

Maybe you've been in similar predicaments, blindsided when a credit card was declined at a business lunch or an impatient landlord cornered you in the elevator. How do we get so out of touch with the money of our businesses?

That's easy—it takes courage to look at the money. Finding out how tight the money really is can be discouraging. And our relationship with money is typically wrapped in fear and ego. We're afraid of being vulnerable if people learn how much we don't know. We're afraid of losing control and losing face.

Besides, that's somebody else's job.

Don't we pay good money to bookkeepers for the very purpose of making sure the bills get paid? We've got smart people all over our money—accountants, CFOs, financial advisors. Why aren't they taking care of us? After all, we didn't go into business to count money. Most of us don't love spending quality time with our spreadsheets.

Dale is pretty typical of owners of small manufacturing companies. What he really likes is selling, building relationships with key accounts. And that's working out pretty well because the company has been successful enough to have others who run the equipment and schedule production and manage distribution.

He sat in my office, sweating over a cash crisis and swearing over the irresponsibility of the bookkeeper who had allowed the crisis to happen. She should've *done* something.

As it turns out, she *had* done something. She'd gone to Dale weeks earlier, warning him that a cash crunch loomed. Maybe he was too anxious to listen or too overworked to take the time. Whatever the case, Dale told her, "Not now. I don't have time for that today. I'm busy trying to earn a living."

Lifeblood Plus

The Flash Report can be used in any business, but is critical in emerging and high-growth businesses where cash can be volatile.

When insufficient revenue caught up with Dale, the bookkeeper took the heat.

Here's a little-known fact for every business owner who prefers the head-in-the-sand method of cash management: Bookkeepers do not manufacture money.

Owners like Dale feel blindsided and betrayed and self-righteously indignant when they're caught with their eyes off the money. And it happens to all of us. Asset Builders, too, have had their share of unpleasant surprises around money. The hard lesson they've learned is that ownership is always accountable for monitoring the money.

Asset Builders keep their eyes on the money.

Down and dirty

Keeping our eyes on the money isn't rocket science. It doesn't take hours and hours. It doesn't even require a special affinity for numbers or advanced training.

In fact, it takes me about 10 minutes once a week.

I'm not a CPA. I wanted something simpler than poring over a balance sheet and trying to calculate what it was telling me. So, like the classic entrepreneur, once I saw the need, I figured out a better and more efficient way to do it. I've identified a process that gives me a weekly one-page look at the current state of certain financial metrics of my business. I've structured these down-and-dirty financial reports in a way that reveals the key information clearly and quickly. So quickly, in fact, that I call it a Flash Report. In about the time it takes to review and sign checks each week, a well-constructed Flash Report gives me a real-time financial snapshot of the business, including short-term cash flow trends from the previous week.

The other vital financial tracking tools are the income statement and the balance sheet.

The balance sheet gives me an accurate monthly picture of my cash balances, my payables and receivables balances and the amount of debt I owe. It tells me the accounting net worth of my business (a different measure from the market net worth of my company) each month.

An income statement is a basic scorecard on critical performance indexes of the business—revenue, gross profit, key expenses and net profit.

Lifeblood Plus

Eagle Eye

Wealth Builders who keep an eagle eye on the money:

- produce and review financials monthly;
- organize financials around revenue, gross profit, cost of goods sold, general administration/overhead and net profit;
- dissect revenue streams using separate profit centers within the business for the purpose of pinpointing opportunities and threats;
- use financial statements to track money trends using monthly, quarterly and annual comparatives;
- work with an external board of advisors who understand and focus on company financials.

This reads like Money 101 for business owners, I know. And it is. But for Asset Builders, this is anything but elementary. They view these commonplace financial reports through a different lens. They aren't just making sure the bills get paid and the customers don't get too far behind. They use financial reports to take care of the short term while planning for the long term. Asset Builders make a discipline of reviewing financial reports and piecing together a comprehensive picture. Financial reporting is the source of the insights they need to make prudent decisions around the use of the company's lifeblood resource of money.

A system of monthly financial disciplines and a thorough knowledge of how to interpret and use them put the business owner in control of the engine that drives economic health.

Lifeblood Plus

1-2-3 Financial Reporting

1. Flash report: a down-and-dirty weekly report on key financial metrics of the business

2. Income statement: a monthly overview of cost of goods sold, over-head and net profit

3. Balance sheet: an accurate score-card of retained earnings and the equi-ty position of the business

---

Following the money trail

Taken together, I use financials to spot problems before they become crises, to make adjustments that can improve the numbers and to arrive at informed decisions. I can track sources of revenue. I can set prices with this information; establish budgets; react more quickly to changes in the marketplace; pinpoint problems earlier.

Here's the trail of money I follow:

Top-line revenue: I look first at the income statement for last month's revenue. This is an important number and I pay close attention to it. But taken in isolation, top-line revenue can lull me into a false sense of security. I never celebrate until I follow the trail to the end, where I learn whether there's something left over.

Revenue sources: If all the revenue goes into one pot, I'll miss key information about the financial picture of my company. When my companies have multiple sources of revenue, I need to know how each income stream is performing. The definitive application of this principle leads to the actual break-out of business units, each with its own budget, revenue and expenses. But even the simpler process of tracking different revenue streams tells me where revenue is being generated and how much is being generated in each area. Broken down this way, the income statement tells me where the organization is underperforming or missing opportunities. It gives me information that I can use for strategic decision-making about where to invest the resources of my company.

Cost of goods sold: Now I'm inching up on the truth about my numbers. What does it cost to get a product or service out the door and into the hands of customers and clients? Supplies, materials, equipment, maybe delivery, sometimes labor, sales expenses—all the hard costs that are absolutely necessary to produce a product or service must show up on the

Lifeblood Plus

The Flash Report

One of the first tools we provide for our clients is the Flash Report, a customizable document designed to give them key financial information each week. The particular categories of information might be different for each business and each owner.

Some of the metrics a Flash Report might contain include:

- Cash balances
- Receivable balances
- Payables balances
- Receivables aging
- Line of Credit (LOC) balances
- LOC availabilities
- Customers who are most significantly past due

income statement. Now I'm beginning to understand what I need to do more of and what I need to do less of.

Gross profit: This is where I draw conclusions about all the numbers I've reviewed. What's left when I subtract cost of goods sold from top-line revenue in each profit center? Is it enough to support a healthy business? The true story of the company's financials begins to emerge.

Overhead: Financial guys call it G&A, or General and Administrative. Most business owners just think of it as the necessary evil of overhead: what does it cost to support the business of the business? If overhead is a

FLASH REPORT

ACCOUNTING

BANK ACCOUNT BALANCES

CHECKING +	$	153,428.55
FLEX SPENDING	$	1,722.97

GROSS SALES

MONTH-TO-	$	88,846.24
YEAR-TO-DATE	$	752,847.07
LAST MONTH	$	163,556.81
LAST YEAR	$	1,072,376.25
2012 PROJEC-	$	1,593,601.99

ACCOUNTS RECEIVABLE

CURRENT	$	285,578.24
LAST FLASH	$	279,519.29
>60 DAYS OLD	$	30,815.00
% > 60 DAYS OLD		11%

ACCOUNTS PAYABLE

CURRENT	$	9,227.10

SALES

SALES DEPT SALES

MONTH-TO-	$	29,294.99

CALLS

MONTH-TO-	236
MONTH-TO-	124

PROSPECTS

CURRENT	$	60,500.00
NEXT MONTH	$	-
TOTAL	$	60,500.00

four-letter word for some business owners, it's only because of how easily it can snowball. When I deduct this number from the gross profit, it takes me to the next number in the money trail.

Net profit: What's left over to work with when it's all said and done? Without net profit, I can't make improvements or growth moves. Over the long haul, this number tells me this machine's potential for building value.

Lifeblood Plus

The Money Trail

Examine your weekly, monthly, quarterly or annual financial statements in this sequence to understand the status of your cash position and your profits.

Top-line revenue
↓
Revenue sources
↓
Cost of goods sold
↓
Gross profit
↓
Overhead
↓
Net profit
↓
Cash flow
↓
Trends on the spreadsheet

Cash flow: Does it? Or is the trickle so slow that the only way to get by is to tap lines of credit? Is the flow dammed up with accounts receivable that are aging beyond the terms of our agreements? Could be cash flow has become a real gusher, spewing out money the minute it comes through the door. Cash is king and if it isn't flowing in faster and more steadily than it's flowing out, I have a problem. Maybe I need to set better customer terms. Maybe I'm too aggressive with payables. Maybe I need to pay more attention to my clients' satisfaction level. Maybe I need better collections procedures. My minimum goal is to fund the business on each month's cash flow. I can't know if that's possible until I've examined the whole picture.

One payoff for funding the business on cash flow, not sales revenue or debt, is that I pay closer attention to the business's highest priorities when it's time to allocate resources.

Trends on the spreadsheet: This month's numbers are important. But taken out of context they may not provide me with the real story. I drop the numbers into a spreadsheet that allows me to compare this month's numbers with last month's and last quarter's and last year's. That spreadsheet makes it easy to see the trends that tell me where the business is headed. Sometimes I recognize opportunities we can capitalize on. Often I spot problems before they go on too long and become crises. This month's information is important; the long view of the broader picture is critical.

That's the money trail I follow. How about you? Are your eyes on the money? If they aren't, how can you be sure that you're making any?

The first time I reached a quarter of a million dollars in revenue in one of my early companies, I had no idea how to read financial statements. No idea what depreciation was. No sense of financial ratios or retained earnings. All I understood was accounts receivable and cash on hand and how much I owed. If I can learn to follow the money trail, anyone can.

It takes courage to look that unflinchingly at the business's finances. But it's not an option if we're playing the Smart Money game.

Lifeblood Plus

Accrual vs. Cash Accounting

Cash accounting recognizes revenue when it is collected and expenses when they are paid. Modified cash accounting recognizes certain non-cash expenses such as depreciation.

Accrual accounting recognizes revenue when it is earned and expenses when they are incurred.

Accountants generally consider accrual accounting to be a more accurate picture of the business's profitability at any point in time because it accounts for all of a company's transactions, whether or not money has changed hands.

Here's the danger for the owner who's following the money trail: money that is earned but never collected negatively affects the cash flow. And if we use projected revenue for decisions about the use of capital, we are operating with funny money. It isn't real money until we have cash in hand.

Asset Builders know instinctively what the flow of money in and out of the business looks like from one week to the next—but they don't rely solely on instinct. They make a point of following the money trail so they know exactly what's been billed, who has paid and who hasn't, when more is going out than they have coming in.

Cash is the lifeblood of the business. Asset Builders know that and pay attention to it as if it were a life-or-death matter. Because it is.

Ownership Perspective

1. Do you have fears about money that make you take your eyes off the money?

2. When you think about the checks and balances to protect the life-blood of the business, do you feel secure?

3. Who really knows the numbers of your business? Do the people making decisions about your money care as much about it as you do?

Smart Money Rule #3
Make Cash Flow

*Cash flow is the vehicle for turning the source
of financial predictability—revenue—
into the fruit of financial sustainability—profit.*

Chapter Seven
Smart Money Rule #3:
Make Cash flow

"Cash is hard to get hold of and harder to hold onto.
It' nature is to flow right through our hands, an always-moving target."

When I was ten years old, my best friend Joey was the richest kid I knew.

Joey had a paper route. Some might not view that as the most lucrative vehicle for a savvy entrepreneur. But Joey could always fund a trip to The Shake Shop, so I knew he was rich.

Everywhere Joey went, he carried a blue book, his official paper route ledger. Whenever we were overtaken by an overpowering craving for ice cream, Joey would pull out his ledger, knock on a door, smile engagingly and tell his customers that it was time to collect on their subscription. Whoever answered the door would hand over a few dollars and we'd go buy a quart of ice cream.

Could be that was when my desire to be an entrepreneur was born.

One Saturday, I learned the lesson of not paying attention to cash flow. I'd spent the night at Joey's and we were getting ready to launch into our weekend. Then Joey heard someone at the front door and got a funny expression on his face.

"Mr. Carson's here," Joey said, dropping his voice to a whisper. "Let's hide."

Mr. Carson was the manager of the paper boys. He'd come to collect for Joey's route. The money Joey had collected from his customers, of course, had already been used to purchase other necessities. So Joey and I hid behind the couch and listened to his mother and Mr. Carson unravel the truth about Joey's cash flow management issues.

I didn't hang around for the meeting with the capitalist who would bail Joey out of his financial difficulties. That last thing I heard as I hightailed it out the door was the ominous warning, "Wait till your dad comes home."

> **The Owner's Voice**
>
> *"I've been in business since 2002. And up until 2008 the business was growing...2009 was by far the worst financial year of my business (and personal) life. Since 2010 I've seen it slowly coming back. And this year is actually my best year ever. I attribute it to 'cutting the fat' from my business and working smarter and longer."*

That was my first real lesson in the dangers of confusing revenue with profit, and the cash flow problems that can follow.

A moving target

What, exactly, is cash flow?

The very words describe our dilemma. Cash is hard to get hold off and harder to hold onto. Its nature is to flow right through our hands, an always-moving target.

In trying to gain a clear picture of the dynamics of cash flow as a major component of the lifeblood of a business, I've come to realize that cash flow isn't a definable thing as much as it is a process. A process, by the way, that looks and operates a little differently in every business.

As owners, we tend to focus our obsession on three main money categories: revenue, profit and cash flow. They tend to fuse in our thinking. Revenue is down, so of course profit will take a hit and we're bound to run into a cash flow crunch. In actuality, these three financial metrics are interconnected but completely separate measurements of our financial health.

One of the problems we, as owners, create with the lifeblood of our business is that we tend to be biased in favor of one metric or another. But the three are interdependent. The health of one depends on the health of all.

The key to robust lifeblood is the main artery that connects 1) the source of financial health—revenue—and 2) the management of our financial health—cash flow—and 3) the fruit of our financial health—profit. Remember, a portion of our revenue always streams into paying expenses. Profit is the portion we get to keep. At that point *profit can either be harvested or it can remain in motion as the raw material from which sustainable economics can be built.*

To put it succinctly, revenue moves into the cash flow process and, if the flow is successful over the long haul, a portion of it may become profit.

If cash flow is a process, when does it begin, when does it end and what happens in between? How do we protect that process so it can best result in the end product of profit?

Lifeblood Plus

Working Capital

Working capital is the portion of every dollar of revenue that must be reinvested to produce a new dollar of revenue. Here's how to figure it.

Current assets

(assets that will convert to cash over the next 12 months)

minus

Current liabilities

(payables plus debt that must be paid in the next 12 months)

equals

Your working capital

Trickling in, gushing out

For most businesses, the cash flow process begins the moment we can bill a customer or client. The cash flow process continues through the point of collection, and concludes when some or all of it funnels into working capital. If anything is left, we call it profit.

Sounds pretty straightforward. But we all know how many variables are at work within that process.

First, do your billings always go out on time? Mine don't. No matter how hard we work at it, things get in the way. Somebody has to pick up a sick kid at school. Holidays happen. The billings go out late.

Second, is there sometimes a lag between the verbal agreement and the signing of a contract? Maybe the guy who has to sign is out of town or

---

Lifeblood Plus

The Cash Flow Quiz

How would your leaders answer the following questions?

- When profits are down, do you have the information necessary to know whether to raise prices or cut costs?
- Do you know which of your company's products or services are the most profitable?
- Are you investing resources in products that don't contribute positively to the bottom line?
- Are your profit margins healthy? Does your pricing structure allow you to give good service and still make a profit?
- How long will it take to achieve a return on investment in a new product or project?
- How much of your budget is fixed overhead and how much of it is variable overhead?
- Do you carefully dissect the costs attached to production so it is possible to track indirect costs such as transportation or delivery?
- When you plan key moves or major initiatives, do you calculate the impact across the organization when calculating ROI?

---

somebody forgets to deliver the contract. I'm certainly guilty of letting that happen. But it's only a few days. How bad can that be?

Do customers seem to think that "payable on receipt" means they are supposed to take a couple of weeks to stroke a check? What do your collections procedures look like? Does the money get to the bank before the close of the banking day or does another day get added to the process?

One of our financial advisors calls all these seemingly minor delays the hidden days in the billing cycle. In the best case scenario, hidden days may number only one or two. If that happens often enough, we'll feel the impact sooner or later. In the worst case, we could be looking at a couple of weeks. When that happens, the impact is major.

Lifeblood Plus

The Trail of Lifeblood

The trail of lifeblood of your business is found by following cash as it flows through your company, from point of contract to collection. That trail begins with the sale and the negotiation of terms that allow for favorable cash flow and continues through every system and process in the business. The speed and efficiency with which money moves from the first billable day through collection and ultimate deployment—that is the lifeblood trail.

Of course, while all those little glitches are slowing down the flow of money in, what's happening to the flow of money going out?

Do your employees forego payday when the admin's kid goes home from school sick? Not at my company. Is the payment on your term note for capital equipment due on the same day every month even when your client is out of town and can't sign checks on time? Maybe the purchasing clerk wants to cross something off his list and orders materials two weeks early. The money is going out steadily whether it's coming in or not. So cash may be trickling in on one end and gushing out at the other.

But, hey, it's just a few days. Right?

Cash flow is a sensitive metric. Even the smallest change can have huge impact on cash flow.

Perry's company is a $16 million business, a service business that has been healthy enough to acquire more than one of its competitors. On any given day, this company's accounts receivable ranges from $1.7 to $1.9 million. By shortening collection time by one day, this business stood to realize up to $45,000 in additional cash flow every quarter.

Perry was stunned as he contemplated what he could accomplish by freeing up an additional $45,000 every quarter. Needless to say, the next day he set changes in motion.

We're not all looking at receivables in the millions. But wouldn't it be interesting to know how improving our collection time by a couple of days might impact the flow of cash through our business?

Lifeblood Plus

***Cash Flow Risks
in a Tough Economy***

- Customers who try to make suppliers and vendors their banks.

- Over-dependence for cash flow on a single source customer, who then has the power to control margins.

- No diversity in banking and lending partners

- Increased probability of employee impropriety as money pressures hit harder—in other words, stealing.

And shouldn't we all know about certain factors that drive the cash flow of our business and what those factors are doing to the lifeblood of our business? Improving these cash flow drivers typically results in a high return with a relatively low investment of resources. The three cash flow drivers are:

- Accounts receivable

- Inventory (when applicable)

- Accounts payable

Clearly, the impact of these drivers varies from business to business. Retail, for example, is almost never affected by accounts receivable but is certainly impacted by inventory. A service company won't be dealing with inventory headaches but typically struggles with aging accounts receivable. And the more narrow your margins, the less room you have for poor cash management and the greater the potential for significant impact.

But every business could improve its cash flow by increasing efficiencies in one or more of these areas.

Focusing on the process

Business owners get testy when cash flow is anemic. Some of us try to fix cash flow problems by tearing people's heads off. While that may seem satisfying in the moment, I don't think I've ever seen it solve the problem. That isn't to say that the people of your organization aren't a part of the solution.

Making cash flow the king in our enterprise requires getting our leaders focused on making the necessary changes that support and improve cash flow drivers.

1. Use weekly flash reports to keep all eyes on the money. (See Chapter 5 for a sample flash report.)

2. Set concrete objectives for improving key measurables and make someone accountable for each objective.

3. Build systems, procedures and an action plan for achieving each objective.

4. Clearly set cash flow terms with customers, with contracts and systems to support and reinforce those terms.

Remember, ownership models the standard for keeping the company's mindset on money. Your leaders will follow your example of

---

Lifeblood Plus

Retail cash flow

Inventory and accounts payable are the cash flow drivers in retail. Cash flow begins either at the time of the sale or at the time you must pay for the goods, whichever comes first. So you can easily fall into a pattern of operating with a negative cash flow if you don't have the clout or the negotiating skills to establish favorable terms with suppliers and wholesalers. Steps to improve the cash flow drivers will be vastly different from one establishment to another with most solutions being customized.

---

understanding the way cash flows through the business and the ripple effects most of us overlook.

In the story of the lifeblood of your business, cash flow is king. If revenue can't be processed and managed efficiently enough to produce the end product of profit, the lifeblood of the business will never be robust. As business owners, we're only as good as our ability to affect cash flow as the vehicle for carrying the lifeblood of our business.

Ownership Perspective

1. What is the hardest part of your role of keeping your company's cash flowing? Who can and should help you share this burden?

2. In your personal life, are you a spender, a saver or an investor of your money? Do you treat the resources of your business like you do your personal resources?

3. How would your decision-making change if you really believed that every decision you make in the business impacts the flow of your money and the wealth potential of your business investment?

Smart Money Rule #4

Avoid the Debt Sinkhole

*When we gamble with debt,
the stake is our freedom.*

CHAPTER EIGHT
SMART MONEY RULE #4:
AVOID THE DEBT SINKHOLE

"The borrower is servant to the lender."

What's your boat worth to you? Your BMW? Your house on the lake?

Are they worth your freedom?

I've seen owners make choices about badges of success that put their freedom at risk. Most of them had no idea they were jeopardizing their freedom for the sake of possessions and stuff. When the recession hit and business slowed down, banks changed the money rules we'd all been living by for years. Margin pressures hit. And there was no way to serve the debt that had for so long been considered business as usual.

We started to realize the toys we'd bought had no balance sheet value. They were not investments.

The same debt became harder to manage because we had to pay it off with the declining margins of our revenue...or, if we were lucky, with the reserves we'd built up so diligently in better years.

What we had once seen as normal debt suddenly had us realizing, oh, wow, we may have to go into *more* debt!

Bankers now wanted to drop by, take a look at our books. We weren't sleeping well…or at all. The fight to get out of debt would be harder and longer. Debt had taken on a life of its own.

Welcome to the Debt Sinkhole.

A few weeks ago I sat with a prominent business man, a blue blood in business who had followed in the footsteps of generations of prominent business men in his community. We exchanged pleasantries about our children and our wives. When I asked him how things had been going for him, he said, "You know, Sam, I'm here. I'm a survivor."

Then, with a humble smile, he laid out his story for me.

About a year earlier, the day after he waved goodbye to his son who was starting college, he woke up to discover the repo man in his driveway. "My first thought was had the neighbors seen. My second thought was how would I get to work. Then it really hit. What would I say to my wife?"

What he realized was that he would have to dig deep into a well of strength and will to survive what was in front of him.

The Owner's Voice

"I've gone back to the basics of focusing on profit and less risk. It feels good to see the bottom line grow and have zero debt."

He did, too. He had been devastated and humiliated but he refused to let it take him down. He still had the wellspring of skills, despite the fact that his industry had changed vastly. Because of his experience—and no doubt because of the social capital he'd earned over decades of doing business in his community—he was able to adapt in the changed business climate.

At our core, most business owners are freedom seekers. We don't want anyone else to control our destiny. When I talk with business owners about their original impetus for becoming entrepreneurs, the most common theme is freedom.

Without realizing it, we allowed debt to become integral to our business model. Debt was no longer just our ticket to the symbols of rich and powerful, it became a way to manage cash flow issues. We were on the fast track to debt. And debt is a slippery slope to loss of freedom.

Debt as a solution to cash flow problems was once as American as apple pie. But most of us are now acutely aware of the consequences of financing tomorrow's dream with today's debt.

The need for debt will not go away. But we have learned to use it differently, and prudently, as a tool and not as an entitlement.

Slaves to debt

The first time I met Nancy was at her home in an exclusive neighborhood of 6,000 square foot homes where most folks had rooms full of designer furnishings and a boat docked at the private marina.

Nancy had called me to talk about her business, so I was on task. We went straight to her home office—a fully stocked bar was nearby and the lake was visible from the picture window—so we could talk about the pain of the business.

The Owner's Voice

"I am accelerating personal debt retirement and plan to sell all businesses within 10 years."

The pain came down to this: She had lost her freedom. She wanted it back. But she was so buried in debt she saw no way out.

Nancy had paid with her freedom for the trappings of a certain lifestyle. The debt monster demanded to be fed, even at the expense of her health, her marriage, the stability of her business. She had become a slave to her possessions. More than once, Nancy said to me, "I'd sell everything I have to get my freedom back."

She had learned the hard way how easy it is to get into debt and how hard it is to get out of debt.

Today, Nancy doesn't live in that house. She owns her home outright in a more modest neighborhood. Her life is simpler, with fewer trappings. She lives debt free. Today she is an Asset Builder and the changes she made a decade ago have enabled her to ride out the rough waters of the Great Recession.

Good debt, bad debt

Don't get me wrong. Debt has its place. Many of us, as early-stage entrepreneurs, needed to jump-start our businesses with some degree of debt, which we usually secured with our own collateral, the promise of future stock options or a promissory note. And many of us, including me, have said to ourselves in recent years, "I've got to do this to stay in the game."

Here's how one savvy owner used debt to stabilize for the long haul when he realized the economy would not be bouncing back in a quarter or even in a year. He and his wife had considerable equity in the home they built a dozen years ago. As soon as the recession hit and it was apparent that real estate would take a significant hit, they pulled money from their equity line. Not to support a lifestyle, but to get every bit of liquidity they could out of the house and into a place where they could access it if needed.

Essentially today they rent their house from the bank, instead of watching it swallowed up by the Debt Sinkhole.

At all stages, debt may be a reasonable alternative for capitalizing an opportunity to take the business to its next level—expanding a facility that

---

Lifeblood Plus

Good Debt/Bad Debt

Good debt	Bad debt
Capital equipment that will provide a return	Latest & greatest technology
	Customer financing
Facilities for growth*	Office image
Key player acquisitions	Employee loans
A roll-up acquisition	Cars for owner's kids

*But don't buy it; be careful about putting your money in the ground, where it isn't necessarily as liquid as you need it to be.

---

would otherwise impede growth or upgrading equipment that no longer keeps pace with industry standards or hiring the player who will elevate your game. That can be an appropriate use of the tool of debt.

The standard to use when gauging whether you're contemplating good debt or bad debt is ROI. Will there be a return on the investment? What will the ROI be? When can you expect that ROI?

If the answer to those questions doesn't justify the expense and the added price tag of debt, don't kid yourself. This debt is not financing an investment.

Debt becomes a sinkhole when we use it to dig our way out of a hole we've already dug. When we're using it to buy time to avoid tough decisions about layoffs or other cost-saving measures. When we can barely afford the payment, but have all the confidence in the world that we're holding the winning lottery ticket. When we have no idea how we'll ever get it paid off. When the cost of losing is too high. That's bad debt, waiting to swallow us up.

Lifeblood Plus

Rules of the Old Economy

The six best rules our parents knew about debt:

1. Set aside 10% of every dollar earned. No exceptions.

2. Live within your means.

3. Pay your bills on time.

4. Earn the right to invest in growth.

5. Secure a profit in every transaction.

6. **These rules never change.**

Sometimes, however, hurricanes hit. Things break down. Extraordinary circumstances don't allow us to live within these rules. When the rules are violated there will be consequences and that can cause us distress. The goal should be to recalibrate to the rules and get back on track.

Inexperienced entrepreneurs who view debt as just another way to pay the bills are especially susceptible to runaway debt. Entrepreneurs who haven't yet sweated over payroll month after month often don't fully respect how hard it is to make the real money necessary to pay for using the funny money. Credit cards, once a rite of passage or a hedge against the unexpected, have become an expectation and a convenience.

Calculated use of debt is one of the practices that make experienced entrepreneurs disproportionately successful as second- and third-round owners—they've often seen the sinkhole up close and personal. They know the risks firsthand and they've learned to watch their step around debt.

Lifeblood Plus

The Smart Money Debt Strategy

- Always operate from strength.
- Use debt for the sure thing, not the gamble.
- Never use business debt to serve a lifestyle.
- Develop a concrete strategy for paying off debt.

The dot-com implosion illustrates what can happen when easy debt is used by inexperienced entrepreneurs who have never learned to earn.

About fifteen years ago, I was lunching with a young dot-com entrepreneur, high on the vision of his future as a multimillionaire. He had sought and received a ton of investment capital. To him, that equaled a successful business. I suggested that his future hinged not on how much money he could raise but how much money he could earn by developing a service or product people were willing to buy at a price that delivered a profit.

"You're living in the old economy," he told me. "Wake up and join the future."

He went bust when the dot-com bubble burst. He had to learn the hard way that being able to borrow capital didn't equal being able to earn a profit.

I vacillate between feeling vindicated and feeling regret that I couldn't convince him that investment capital, received and handled too offhandedly, could easily become just another form of debt that could pull him under.

When it comes to the fundamentals, the "old economy" rules are as valid today as they were 50 years ago.

Staying afloat

When facing the debt decision, today's choices may determine whether the bank is running your show tomorrow. What can we learn from business owners whose freedom has been buried under debt?

Diving in is easier than climbing out. Business owners, even in today's capital-scarce market, sometimes attract significant players who have incentive to give us debt. It's so easy, and so tempting, to say "yes" to money when we need it. Let's not forget why all those lenders are willing to loan us their money: when we do, we work for them. After Uncle Sam, the next slice of every dollar we earn goes to our lenders. A piece of wisdom from the book of Proverbs tells us, "The borrower is servant to the lender." Always has been, always will be.

The Asset Builder knows that we work for the lender until the debt is paid off. That makes the borrower the employee and the banker the boss. No wonder the biggest buildings in most cities are financial institutions. *I owe, I owe, so off to work I go.* No thanks.

Use debt for the sure thing, not the gamble. Pursue untested concepts with earnings, not with debt. Risks are inherent to building enterprise. But the riskier the move, the more fiscally conservative we

---

Lifeblood Plus

Banking Buddies

I love the fairy tale that we can make friends with our bankers and thus write our own ticket when the time comes to borrow. Maybe that still happens in small towns. But in many markets, the players in banking come and go quickly. So the banker relationship you cultivate today may not exist next week. Only at the top will you find more stability. That's where to spend your energy building relationships. I don't know a business owner who hasn't had a moment of bonding with a banker over a cup of coffee, a lunch and a peek at those financials—just to make sure those owners are happy with the bank's services, of course.

---

should be in financing it. Asset Builders earn the right to make bold moves. They fund with debt only when they have an ace in the hole.

Never use business debt to serve a lifestyle. This doesn't mean we can't reap rewards of our hard-won success. When the business can afford to reward us—and the other players who have made the rewards possible—we should reap some reward. But Asset Builders know that lifestyle can be a bottomless pit.

If lifestyle becomes our priority, no matter how much we buy today, it won't be enough to satisfy us tomorrow. And lifestyle never pays dividends. So when we finance it with debt, we're waving that money goodbye.

Develop a strategy for paying off debt. Too often we sign on the dotted line, cash the check and only think of the debt once a month when we make another payment. Borrowed money should make possible increased profits that not only boost the bottom line, but also provide the money to repay the debt. If debt only allows us to stay above water today, all we've done is dig a deeper sinkhole.

To stay afloat when we borrow, we need a realistic plan for repayment, starting by resolving the circumstances that led to the need for debt in the first place.

Always operate from strength. Business owners make the mistake of waiting until they need money before they try to secure it. Bankers and other capitalists have no respect for need. Need is weak and they aren't eager to invest in weakness. When you go to lenders in times of financial famine, terms will be structured overwhelmingly in their favor and you'll pay dearly for whatever crumbs they're willing to risk. In today's risk-averse marketplace, nobody doubts that.

The Asset Builder calculates cash needs well in advance by forecasting the numbers, anticipating capital needs and lining up the resources while the company looks strong, with a compelling story to tell and a sense of optimism. When possible, establish lines of credit whether you need them or not. Establish them even if you have no intention of tapping them.

Let me tell you about an Asset Builder I know who understands how to use debt to improve his financial position and give the banks a run for their money at the same time.

Ed was about three years into a start-up. He had a small staff, a small office, a small client base. And a big line of credit.

When he first opened his office, Ed went to the bank where he'd been doing business for years. Over the years, he's made a point of getting to know all the bankers—and the people they report to—by their first names. So the decision-makers he approached were like old friends; they trusted him and knew he had always proven to be a good risk. He outlined his plan for them and asked for a line of credit.

The bankers were impressed. He didn't need their money and bankers love to give their money to people who already appear to have money.

Ed, they wanted to know, *what's your collateral? Should we use your house?*

Lifeblood Plus

The High Cost of Debt

How would I describe the yoke of debt?

- Sleeplessness

- Anxiety

- Short-sightedness

- Lack of innovation

- Weak negotiation power

- Lack of hope

- A sense of powerlessness

In the end, it's all about freedom.

No, that wasn't really what Ed had in mind. Ed wanted to separate the business finances from his personal finances. Couldn't he guarantee the line of credit with his signature? After all, they'd known him for years. He'd always paid what he owed, when he owed it. If that didn't work for them, well, it wasn't like he needed the money. Maybe he'd just wait.

So, of course, the bankers established a line of credit for Ed.

A few months later, Ed went to another banker he'd met through one of his clients and took out a loan. He used that loan to pay off the line of credit, which improved his standing with the first bank. Some time after that, Ed began to build a relationship at a third bank. Eventually, Ed had unsecured lines of credit totaling $250,000 available to him whenever he needed it.

"I didn't need the credit," Ed said. "I just wanted to create a little elasticity in my available credit. Every time I paid off a loan or a line of credit, my bankers increased the credit available to me. They were actually competing for my business."

Sometimes Ed even uses the money his bankers are so eager to lend him. But only when he knows exactly how his finances are going to line up in the near future to allow him to pay it off. And only when the money is being used to make his company better in some way.

Ed's business was immature in many ways. But Ed showed all the earmarks of an Asset Builder in the making.

Asset Builders learn the right times and the right reasons to go into debt, as well as the right strategies for handling debt. Debt doesn't have to be the enemy if we make calculated choices instead of desperate, reckless or uninformed decisions. In fact, when viewed as a bloodline providing flexible access to liquid capital, prudent debt can be part of an Asset Builder's capital plan.

It's not prudent or reasonable to declare that we should avoid debt at all costs. But failure to manage it strategically is a significant threat to the healthy flow of the lifeblood of our business. And remember, when you gamble with debt, your freedom is at stake.

Ownership Perspective

1. Where are you vulnerable to becoming mired in debt?

2. In the recalibration of the economy in recent years, what have been the lessons of debt and exposure that you've carried forward as part of your new plan?

3. What safeguards do you have in your life to insure against bad money decisions?

Smart Money Rule #5

Hedge Your Bets

Every failure traces back to a false assumption.

CHAPTER NINE
SMART MONEY RULE #5:
HEDGE YOUR BETS

"Unsupported guesswork can deal a mortal blow."

The things we don't know can kill us.

Every day, business owners are compelled to step into the unknown. Business is fraught with far-reaching decisions that must be made before we have enough wisdom or experience or data to understand the full impact of our choices. If they taught us nothing else, surely the events of 2001 and 2008 taught us how easy it is to be blindsided by events few could imagine.

But we can't be paralyzed by the fact that each day we're walking out into the unknown. Sometimes all we can do is make a leap of faith.

Everything about owning a business is risky. Starting a business is a risk. Growth is a risk. Selling or merging or expanding—all are risks. Every decision and every move become risky when the neck that's on the line is ours. Can we afford to hire that key player? Can we afford to upgrade our technology? Can we afford not to? Not taking those risks can be the biggest risk of all. A business driven by fear will stagnate. And a stagnant business will die.

We can't be business owners without dealing with the risks. Take enough risks and we're bound to lose a bet here and there.

And what we risk when we lose a bet is always significant. We risk revenue. We risk the livelihood of people who depend on us. We risk the kids' college fund. We risk our freedom and our pride. Often, if we've signed personal guarantees for contracts or lines of credit, we risk our homes. The stakes are high, all the money on the table is ours and nobody wins every hand.

So we make assumptions. We rely on the lessons of past experience. We line up our actions against what we believe to be true. If we're smart, we ask questions and listen to the answers. We get advice. But most often we trust our gut because our instincts have typically served us well.

Entrepreneurs have the reputation for being risk takers. In reality, with so much at stake, we're pretty risk averse. So we learn to minimize the risks. We learn to hedge our bets.

Lifeblood Plus

Let's Assume These Are the Laws of Hedging

- The owner with the fewest assumptions and the most facts wins.

- Bad contracts are cement shoes that will take you down.

- Decide whether you can live with the worst case scenario.

- Every employee is an investment...and a gamble.

- Firewall your family finances.

Unsupported guesswork

About 20 years ago, a woman launched a retail venture by renting booth space to diverse vendors with compatible and related wares. Her assumption was that buyers would be attracted to an atmosphere where they could engage in the same kind of thrill-of-the-hunt that attracts die-hard antiquers.

That assumption proved to be true.

A few years later, exhilarated by her success and looking to diversify her portfolio, she decided to buy a clothing boutique. She assumed that, because she had succeeded in her first retail venture, she could transfer what she'd learned to operating this boutique.

That assumption proved to be wrong.

The customer base was different, the product was different, the venue itself was different. The basic formula that had worked in the original enterprise didn't transfer to the new store.

The price tag for this faulty premise ran into seven figures. I met this woman about 10 years later,. Her once robustly profitable retail establishment was saddled with $750,000 in debt accrued because of her faulty assumption about a business model that ultimately failed. That failure and the resulting debt were pushing the successful enterprise dangerously close to the edge of failure.

That young woman didn't understand that unsupported guesswork can deal a mortal blow.

Never underestimate the dangers of a false assumption.

Avoiding the mortal wound

Hedging a bet is the art of minimizing exposure while our assumptions are being tested.

In a world where confidence is a prerequisite, false assumptions thrive. We get confident of our judgment and pretty soon we forget we aren't dealing with facts. Somebody said it, so we believe it. Common knowledge becomes solid business intelligence. Estimates become data. Conviction becomes wise counsel. Then we start basing our judgments on information that isn't accurate. A false assumption is born.

Acting on one major false assumption can take a business under— or come close, especially when the price tag for a false assumption can be in the millions. Even an apparently small theory that proves to be wrong can have a big impact on the lifeblood of a business.

101

Here's another example of a simple, understandable false assumption that came with a $50,000 price tag.

Some years ago, the trade show marketing company I had bought as a turnaround had a significant opportunity when one of our national clients wanted a custom exhibit for a major trade show exhibit in Chicago—a big-time venue where the floor marshal Gestapo maintain a highly-regulated environment.

I felt confident that I was on solid ground because I'd put together a team of top-notch craftsmen. Their background was in building store fixtures and I made what I thought was a safe assumption: their skills would transfer to the high-end trade show marketing arena. So I showed up on the trade show floor confident that the installation would go smoothly.

Sadly, my assumption that my production crew had the necessary controls and systems in place to meet the requirements of the customer and the exhibit hall proved to be wrong. Our customer's exhibit was two   inches—that's right, *inches*—too tall—that's right, too *tall*; it wasn't even encroaching on anyone else's territory. Reason said two inches in a 2.2 million-square foot exhibit hall was insignificant. Fire code and show marshals, however, said this high-dollar, custom exhibit had to come down…two inches.

> **The Owner's Voice**
>
> *"We are in control of our destiny. We want to provide for our employees, but at the end of the day, my business partner and I know that if we have to shrink to survive and ultimately grow, we can do it. We are not at the mercy of someone else."*

We disassembled the entire exhibit and trimmed two inches off the top.

That false assumption cost my company $50,000 at a time when we were already fighting to survive on our existing lifeblood. I don't even want to think about what it cost in reputation and customer confidence.

An assumption is nothing more than our best guess about what will happen if we take a certain action: If we hire the heavy hitter, sales will go up. Or: If we raise prices, revenue will go up. Or maybe: If we raise prices, customers will go away. Even: If we move to a bigger facility, productivity will go up or we'll attract a caliber of clientele willing to pay more for our services because we've impressed them with our image.

When we hedge our bets, we're simply taking measures to avoid delivering a mortal wound to the lifeblood of our company if our assumptions turn out to be wrong.

The Big Three gambles

Asset Builders hedge their bets in three key areas of business: people, growth moves and contracted agreements.

People: One of the biggest points of pain for any business is bad personnel moves. Nowhere else in business do we make more false ssumptions. We assume people will be honest, loyal, capable of everything we hired them for. We're blindsided when our golden boy sales rep leaves and takes his relationships with him. We're stunned when a key leader is building a business within our business, spawning competition on our time and our money. Hiring the wrong person, hanging onto the wrong person and trusting the wrong person all cost money and cause disruption.

> ### The Owner's Voice
>
> *"The costs associated with doing business have increased while the ability to compete has also increased, making margins much slimmer. Margin for error must be less or you're done."*

The safe assumption: Every player is a gamble.

Growth moves: Prepare for growth, but don't lunge. It's easier to get poor quick than it is to get rich quick. One big growth move is riskier than a series of small moves, so hedge your bets by planning for growth in stages.

Here's an example. Many of my business owner clients want to expand their company's geographic footprint. Some want to go national—or today, international. Others just want regional presence. Smart ways to make those moves include following a customer who is expanding, giving ourselves a built-in client base; acquiring a smaller operation in the location we want, which avoids the costs and uncertainties of a start-up elsewhere; systematizing and codifying what we do so we can bring in the right player in the right location when circumstances align.

In every case, risk has been minimized, the cost of failure lowered.

The safe assumption: A safer pathway to the unknown is sometimes a familiar, well-traveled trail.

Contracts: A bad contract is like a pair of cement shoes, dragging us down when we get into deep water. Yet we sign them all the time, as we must.—leases, purchase agreements, agreements with customers and vendors.

I'm certainly not advocating a business environment with no commitments. In fact, a good written agreement becomes the basis for trust in our business partnerships. But we're prone to go to contract before we know what our assumptions are and what the consequences will be if our assumptions are wrong.

Sign on the dotted line only when you can live with the worst case scenario outcome. Try to make sure every contract has a back door that you can afford to exit.

The safe assumption: The business owner with the fewest assumptions wins.

Forecasting false assumptions

Unless we're going to be paralyzed by inaction, we must weigh our assumptions every day. The bigger the decision, the greater the impact of a false assumption on the lifeblood of the business. Ironically, a business practice we all rely on is nothing but applying assumptions to the lifeblood of the business: forecasting.

If assumptions are so dangerous, how do we avoid those dangers when we're forecasting our numbers for the months ahead as part of our strategic decision-making process? Forecasting as a disciplined process gives us information against which to measure our assumptions; it also demonstrates how to test other assumptions. We can follow these steps to minimize the assumptions made when forecasting our numbers.

1. Look back before we look forward. Pull as much specific historical data as possible on company financials. Break the numbers down monthly or quarterly; break them down by profit center. The more precise our numbers, the more accurate our projections.

2. Identify our assumptions. And understand that they are assumptions, not facts. When we see consistent patterns of monthly, quarterly or seasonal activity, we have to guard against locking in on one assumption before we've explored all the possibilities. No matter how strong our gut feeling, we must safely assume that we're dealing with at least one false assumption.

3. Separate facts from fiction. Be prudent in estimating what kind of revenue we can count on each month through contractual relationships or customer retention. Factor in every monthly expense. Err on the side of caution. Business owners are optimistic and it's easy to be overly optimistic.

4. Project the numbers. Based on sales history, what is a reasonable expectation for new monthly revenue? What is a likely rate of growth based on history as well as present sales and marketing efforts? What costs will go up this year, including growth-related costs (materials, staffing, equipment, facilities, etc.)? Pull it all together in a pro forma that communicates *what must happen* each month to achieve company goals.

5. Review results. Systematically examine our assumptions against reality. The flash report is a down-and-dirty weekly or bi-weekly reality check. Take a close look once a month. Take a hard look every 90 days. When our business is in a high-risk period, we can step up our timeframe for review. This will allow us to identify our false assumptions earlier. And at each monthly and quarterly review, make sure everybody knows how close we come to the mark.

And always remember, assumptions aren't facts and neither are forecasts.

Testing our assumptions

False assumptions can kill us. But every day in the life of a business owner requires sifting through assumptions to get to the facts and make decisions. We can't avoid assumptions because we can't avoid making decisions.

The best we can do is hedge our bets by minimizing our exposure while we test our assumptions.

Here's an example with a happy ending. Some years ago I had the opportunity to buy a business. It wasn't healthy, not by a long shot; but I made some carefully considered assumptions.

- Assumption 1: I believed I could turn it around and make it profitable.

- Assumption 2: I believed I could redefine the business.

- Assumption 3: I believed I could implement a better sales strategy.

- Assumption 4: I believed the brand was strong enough that I could capitalize on it.

- Assumption 5: I believed I could improve the sales cycle.

- Assumption 6: I believed I could build a successful leadership team.

That's a lot of assumptions. A lot of room for the one false assumption that would mean losing my shirt. With that many assumptions, I knew I needed to seriously limit my exposure, my potential for loss.

First, I had to limit the money I invested.

Second, I had to give myself a back door so I wouldn't lose everything I had invested.

Third, I wanted the option to walk away with no penalties except my own lost time and (limited) investment capital.

I couldn't eliminate all the risks, but I could narrow my assumption base and shift as much risk as possible to the seller.

Here's how it played out. The deal was structured as an option to buy, with a short and specific buy-out date and an agreed-upon price. I put $15,000 on the table, with the understanding that I would pony up another $750,000 if I exercised my right to buy. And I insisted on complete ownership authority while I tried to turn the business around.

I proved my assumptions. When the option period ended, I paid for the business with the retained earnings I had accrued while turning the company around.

If my assumptions had been wrong, the worst-case scenario is that I could have walked away with invaluable experience and out $15,000. However, in this case, eight years later, I sold that company for $3.2 million, netting $1 million in profit.

Hedging our bets won't always net us $1 million in profit. Let me hedge my bets here and say there may even be a day when it won't save us from losing our shirts. But hedging our bets will minimize the times when we need to say, "If I knew then what I know now…" It happens to everyone, but business owners can't afford the luxury of too many false assumptions, any more than they can afford the luxury of waiting until every solution is clear.

Lifeblood Plus

Trust Your Gut and Back It Up with Numbers

Many of us hate forecasting. We'd rather rely on our gut. Our industry is too unpredictable. We don't want to get locked into anything. Some of us are just afraid of saying it and then failing to achieve it.

Asset Builders trust their gut because they've backed it up with numbers. Asset Builders tame the unpredictability of their industry by studying previous years for patterns. Asset Builders can afford to be flexible because they've planned for change.

Then there's that fear of failure. It's true, we may not always hit the numbers we project. But in the process of arriving at those numbers and expressing them to our team, we've given our business a head start on success.

Smart Money players have mastered the art of narrowing their assumptions by testing them. Every assumption they prove or disprove becomes experience which they can leverage to make decisions based on assumptions with less risk. Hedging our bets by leveraging our experience is as close as we can get to a sure-thing.

Ownership Perspective

1. Have you ever experienced an "arrogant moment" when your ego caused you to leap before your checked your assumptions?

2. Where must you constantly check assumptions before making decisions that will impact the lifeblood of your business?

3. Do you know good hedging when you see it? Who do you know in your life who has mastered this *Hedge Your Bet* rule?

Smart Money Rule #6:

Leverage Down

*Under the surface of every business
is untapped gold waiting to be mined.*

CHAPTER TEN
SMART MONEY RULE #6:
LEVERAGE DOWN

"Smart Money never fails, it just evolves."

When it's broken, I don't want to fix it. I want to reinvent it. Innovate. Come up with a better idea to replace the one that isn't yet working perfectly.

Sometimes, that sparks an exciting new chapter in the life of my business. Sometimes it means the business spends hard-earned money on valuable assets that sit idle and under-utilized because I've decided to spend more money to accomplish something we already have the tools to accomplish.

It's part of my nature. In fact, that tendency to leap from one hot idea to the next is part of the entrepreneurial nature I see in almost every business owner. Most of us are visionaries; we love to create. But few of us have the patience to refine. Except for the rare breed of entrepreneur who delights in the painstaking process of seeking perfection in the details, it's against our nature to repeat and repeat until we get it right.

Innovation is on our DNA strand, right there with our survival instinct. We never want to be free of it, but we can't let it undermine execution. And we can't let it blind us to opportunities to increase the value of our business asset at the same time we preserve the lifeblood of the enterprise.

Asset Builders have learned what our prudent mothers tried to tell us years ago: Make the most of what you've been given.

Leveraging down has proven to be my greatest source of wealth and hope in recent years. By taking the library of intellectual capital I've developed on business ownership over the years and making it available to an electronic community, I'm mining the gold of decades of work and finding ways to monetize it.

Sometimes we don't need to innovate; we need to go deep to mine the gold in our organizations. We need to leverage down.

Leverage the assets you already have before you hunt down new ones. Leveraging the gold you have is always cheaper than mining for new gold. And the old vein is usually richer than the new vein.

Soft assets, hard money

Leveraging existing assets isn't as much fun as nailing the next big account or gearing up for the new product that's going to knock everyone's socks off. Leveraging isn't sexy. It doesn't get the adrenaline flowing. It

---

Lifeblood Plus

Leveraging experience

Answer these questions to find out whether you leverage the assets of experience and wisdom.

1. Do you have a board of outside advisors whose experience and objectivity you can leverage?

2. Do you have an identifiable process for evaluating company and individual mistakes in order to learn from them?

3. Do people in your company feel the need to cover up mistakes to avoid blame?

4. Which question does your company ask: *Whose fault is this?* Or *How did this happen and what can we learn from it?*

---

doesn't give us the same satisfaction as watching our leaders scrambling to catch up with us before we come up with the next great idea. No, leveraging our existing assets is not shoot-the-rapids exhilarating.

It's just smart.

Most of us have more assets to leverage than we realize, and we're under-utilizing most of them because we fail to recognize them as assets. Capital equipment? Asset. Product inventory? Asset. Office furnishings? Asset. Intellectual capital? Put that one in the assets column, too.

Let's take a quick inventory of the assets we tend to overlook, assets that don't show up on the P&L, and see if we can't relate them to money in more tangible ways. Most of the assets we under-utilize will fall into two broad categories: talent and wisdom.

The Owner's Voice

"Necessity is the mother of invention, and innovation in my profession is actually more interesting than grinding away for someone else's benefit."

Talent. The typical business spends more money on people than almost any other asset. Yet it isn't putting this talent to its highest and best use. Is the best brain for building systems and procedures screwing up payroll every week because that employee is the easy solution, even though the person is lousy with the books? It's very common to find a company's best sales person overseeing the sales team instead of closing prospects.

It even happens with owners. Some of us are managing people inside the company or overseeing production when we ought to be setting strategy or nurturing key account relationships. Delegation is the greatest tool we have for multiplying our capacity as owners. Yet we squander our greatest talents because we don't teach others how to do what we do. We hang onto the small stuff long past the point when we should've passed it down the line.

In recent years, I've worked with three different owners who were so buried in the work of the business they couldn't get to the work they were uniquely gifted to do.

The first owner drove trucks because he believed he couldn't afford to hire enough drivers to keep the trucks rolling. Of course he couldn't afford drivers. He was the number one sales guy, and he was *driving a truck!* Not only did this make it nearly impossible for him to hunt opportunities, when an opportunity did show up, he missed it because he was too busy shifting gears.

The second owner relished her role as the deal maker. Put her in front of a prospect and she could close the deal. It wasn't unusual for her to have a $10 million deal in her pocket. But the business wasn't prepared to capitalize on the opportunity because it didn't have a CEO. This owner had never raised up a leader who could manage the day-to-day operations; she was paying for the talent, she just wasn't applying it well. When she was playing in the minors, she could handle the two key positions of CEO and key account salesperson. But when the game began to heat up, nobody was warming up in the bullpen to take over the day-to-day for her.

The Owner's Voice

"As we have grown, we have experienced specialization. Instead of being a group of generalists, we now have incredible people doing what they are great at. This allows me to do what I love and lead the organization forward. I believe that feeling less pressure is the result of being solely focused on those things that you are well-suited for."

Owner number three enjoyed the adrenaline rush of his company's rapid-response disaster restoration and repair service so much that he almost missed the chance to franchise his operation when the time was right. He allowed the entire organization to be controlled by the unpredictability of fires, floods and weather-related disasters—everyone was expected to slide down the pole when the fire bell rang. The company could gain no momentum to build the infrastructure and disciplines that franchising would require because all the talent was pulled into crisis and chaos.

When that owner pulled himself out of the fray and became the enterprise architect, his opportunity to franchise took root. He began to leverage the success of his business model through a franchising strategy that duplicates his success one business unit at a time. Today, under a franchise model, he has partners investing in his brand and bringing to the table capital, experience and relationships he can leverage to increase the value of his asset.

Leveraging is not a soft concept. These three owners were paying dearly—in hard dollars and lost opportunities—for the failure to leverage their talent.

Lifeblood Plus

The Freedom to Create

An unintended consequence of the economic shift is the associated fears of loss that cause a contraction of creativity. Yet we need creative thinking more than ever if we are to find fresh pathways to economic health. The best way to leverage the thinking power of our enterprise is to give our people problems to solve instead of solutions to implement.

If we evaluate every key player on our team, whose talent are we wasting because it's expedient or because we feel we don't have another option? And what are we losing when we do so? A player's rich network of contacts? Insights into operational efficiencies? Someone's unique ability to motivate and bring out the best in others? Ultimately, will we lose these players and every penny and every hour we've invested in them because they left for positions that allowed them to work out of their sweet spot?

Here's what has historically work best at my company—making sure every key player is riveted on the one thing he or she is best gifted to contribute to the company. Our managing partner is no longer bogged down in nuts-and-bolts consulting; he's been elevated to high-level interventions, investment banking projects and leading in strategic planning for consulting clients. We have a player whose strength is a systematic, logical approach to problem solving, making him the obvious choice for leading in enterprise architecture. And we have a player whose greatest gift is patience—that's my assistant.

And now that we're all highly focused on the things we do best, the business is executing better than it ever has. I'm leveraging the talent in my company.

What are you doing to leverage the talent you're paying for?

Wisdom. Failing to leverage knowledge, experience and lessons learned should be a capital offense for business owners. Guilty, your honor, of squandering in the first degree, punishable by a slow, painful death.

Every mistake, every failure, every experience, decision and initiative has an ROI—it comes when we evaluate what's happened and apply what we just learned to the next venture. Smart Money never fails, it just evolves. Asset Builders don't look at mistakes like money out of their wallet. Instead, every experience—from miserable failure to unprecedented success—is simply a lesson for which a price was paid. The only real mistake is failing to mine the lessons in order to get closer to success, or to elevate the level of success.

One of the most damaging ways we fail to leverage wisdom and experience is in creating a culture of blame. As the owner we determine whether our companies look for a scapegoat or look for a lesson. When our companies are focused on laying blame, people will cover up their mistakes, making it impossible to improve or avoid those same mistakes in the future.

Lifeblood Plus

The Annual Strategic Planning Event:
Get Honest, Get Focused, Get Fired Up

The most important thing to remember about your company's annual strategic planning event is to avoid a what-the-boss-wants event, where people's eyes glaze over and they laugh at all the right moments. What you want is a thinking event, where people get honest, get focused and get fired up.

Here are the steps to make that happen.

Timing is everything. A new calendar year traditionally marks a time for change, renewal and recommitment. Many companies begin a season of reflection late in the fourth quarter of the year or the first month of the new year.

Set the stage. A week ahead of time, make sure the leaders who will attend have: 1) a copy of last year's written strategic plan, the business plan or other strategic documents that capture where the company thought it was headed

We can keep paying the price for mistakes again and again, or we can get the pay-off for mistakes by using them to drive continuous improvement.

Taking stock

In my work with business owners, we encourage three levels of leveraging the collective wisdom of the organization. Level one is a process to continuously improve execution at 90-day intervals. Level two allows the organization to harvest the gold of an entire year before the greatest successes and the most significant lessons are forgotten. Level three is our personal reflection on our role as owner.

Level 1: The 90-day review. My company has leveraged its experience in building businesses to create an Enterprise Architecture process. The process is driven by a closed-loop system for excellent execution and continuous improvement in our client companies.

Every 90 days, client company leaders evaluate performance against a measurable plan to see what's working and what's not. Based on the

---

when the current year began; 2) probing questions to provoke fresh thinking.

Reflect. Owners and leaders tend to rivet their thinking on tactics and action. When we do, we compromise thinking power. So don't just jump into solutions. Make the first session of your retreat a time to reflect on the highlights of the year just ending.

Ask driving questions. Remember those probing questions distributed the week before the retreat? After reflection, it's time to answer them. What can we do to win the game? What stands in our way? What are the critical functions we must master to win the game? How will the business be different when we do? What will it mean in terms of new roles, new systems, new structure? This is where "we've always done it that way" thinking transforms into innovation and a "that's your problem" mentality shifts to collective problem-solving.

Map out the future. Set reasonable projections for the year ahead and come up with a plan to hit them. Prioritize goals and agree on the best leader for each goal, project or initiative. Write down the plan for the next 90 days and sketch out the three 90-day periods after that.

---

review, plans are improved and refined. Better strategies are employed. Resources may be re-allocated. Faulty assumptions are spotted before they become major crises.

Ninety days at a time, the company improves its strategic thinking and its execution by taking an account of its progress. This simple process is the most effective way to leverage a company's experience.

Level 2: The annual strategic planning event. The most successful businesses make time at the end of each year to step back and mine the golden nuggets from the year just ending. This becomes the natural first step in planning the year ahead. The best way to do this is at an annual strategic event for company ownership and leadership.

We use two tools at our annual strategy sessions that allow companies to gain greater clarity about how the business stands today compared to one year ago. Some companies use our Business Asset Profile year after year, watching the evolution in key areas like sales, marketing, communication, trust,

Lifeblood Plus

Seek wise counsel

We can all benefit from a fresh perspective and the wisdom others gained the hard way. But few of us bring together our trusted advisors to aid us in making difficult and crucial decisions. Most of us have an attorney, an accountant, maybe a financial planner, but their input is typically fragmented and tactical, not part of an integrated strategy. If you don't have a trusted group or board, create one.

use of resources and more. The Business Unit Scorecard provides a measurement of execution, customer relations, innovation and other critical success factors for profit centers of the business. Most companies love the graphs that give tangible proof of their progress from year to year. But what owners love is the enthusiasm and motivation of their leaders when they can track the effects of their work.

In fact, the discipline of an end-of-year strategic event can become a defining moment for the business, empowering its leaders and shifting its focus in ways that are profound and positive. When companies leave our end-of-year events, they launch into the new year with heightened awareness of how to avoid yesterday's mistakes and create tomorrow's successes.

Level 3: Ownership inventory. Our role as owner offers the chance to take stock in unique ways. As the year ends, I like to reflect on my vision for the company. I evaluate how well company directions are aligned with that vision. I determine what I could do more of—and less of—to make progress toward my vision. Setting goals in each area of life— physical, relational, spiritual, mental and professional—greatly increases the probability that I'll actually make the changes I desire.

One of the great values of taking personal inventory as owners is that it brings us back to our very core, enabling us to get down to the essence that was buried by the sometimes overwhelming responsibilities of our roles in the day-to-day of our businesses. This level of inventory reveals our brokenness, allows us to deal with our hubris and our delusions.

In doing so, we come to realize that mistakes are not failures, but material with which to rebuild out of strength as we recalibrate and return to our core.

Value of a good mistake

Every three years, a healthy business transforms itself. That's not a suggestion or speculation, it's a fact. We'll be better or worse, but we'll never remain the same.

The purpose of leveraging our experience is to make certain the business is transforming according to our plan and our vision, not randomly or reactively.

Thomas Watson—not the IBM guy, but the 17th-century theologian who became embroiled in the tug of war between the Anglican and Catholic churches—once said, "If you want to increase the speed of your success, you must increase the rate of your failure."

119

Mistakes create learning opportunities. Learning leads to excellence and excellence always gives a shot in the arm to the lifeblood of the business. Will you capture the capital of your mistakes? Smart Asset Builders know the value of a good mistake.

Ownership Perspective

1. Do you treat intellectual, human and time capital as if it is as valuable as money?

2. In what ways might your drive to create become a hindrance to achieving excellence in execution?

3. Make a list of all the soft assets of your business. Which ones are under-leveraged?

4. What is your natural reaction to mistakes and misfires? What effect does your reaction have on the thinking power of those under your employ?

Smart Money Rule #7

Think Like a Capitalist

*Prepare for the day when an infusion of capital
can elevate the economic potential of the business.*

Chapter Eleven
Smart Money Rule #7:
Think Like a Capitalist

*"The ultimate price of having no capital plan would be
that there is no end in sight to your time on the ownership treadmill."*

Two young business owners were riding high in the heyday of
economic abundance between 9-11 and the fall of 2008. Having worked
together at another firm for several years, they had formed a strong bond as
they sharpened their industry savvy and ultimately founded their own
professional services firm.

Clients loved them. They attracted talent, nailed big accounts and
distributed big year-end profits. They bought some very desirable real estate
for their offices and congratulated themselves on a very smart investment.

And without any experience in the value of equity, they began to use
that equity in their booming enterprise as incentive for holding onto the
best of their talent.

Then the economic landscape began to reshape, and with it, the
demands of their industry.

They needed new technology. They needed talent with a
new-economy mindset. But because they had been distributing profits instead of re-investing them, they did not have the resources to respond to

this new day in the marketplace. Over time, some of their big accounts went away.

But the banks still wanted theirs and the employees still wanted theirs. One of the owners, even, still wanted his. He wasn't willing to risk what he had taken out of the business in order to protect the value of the firm.

The other owner now saw clearly the fatal mistake of having no capital plan.

Cash flow droughts

How seriously you take your role as the capital planner for your business has probably been tested since 2008. Few of us have walked through the Great Recession without confronting the need for additional capital at some point.

So what happened? Was your plan in place, enabling you to tap into what you needed and meet your company's need for cash? Or did your company feel what it was to be starved for oxygen?

Most of us relied heavily on our banks as our investor or capitalist. We had lines of credit to see us through the brief cash flow droughts that

---

Lifeblood Plus

Debunking the Growth Myth

Most business owners I know cherish the myth that growth will solve all their money problems. Who needs a capitalist? We'll just sell more. Get more customers. Make an acquisition. Crank up the volume and our problems will be solved.

In reality, the cost of growth is always more than we ever estimate. And the returns are always slower coming in than we ever estimate.

Few business owners are wired to be the capitalist to their own enterprise through a significant growth phase. And self-capitalizing with profits from the business has never been more precarious because of the tension with limited margin of error. Growth means there is more probability of getting exposed before you can contract and adjust.

---

any business experiences. Many of us had the kind of banking relationships that would allow us to borrow money secured with little more than writing our names on the dotted line or calling our friend Charlie at the bank, if the need arose. And, of course, many of us had our personal estates to tap if a not-to-be-missed opportunity or a one-time setback occurred.

Those days are over. We've been through a period when banks won't renew our LOCs. Our signatures won't get us what they got us a half-dozen years ago, even with the assets of our businesses thrown in for good measure. Many of us have already depleted our personal estates as much as we feel comfortable doing, and then some.

Lifeblood Plus

Is It Time?

What are the telltale signs that a business needs an infusion of outside capital in order to move the business to its next life stage?

- You're dangerously close to failing to meet payroll more than once in any given quarter.

- You feel like the world is on your shoulders.

- Your net worth is threatened every payroll. One hiccup in the supply chain and you're caught holding the cost of of labor or the cost of goods.

- You turn away from growth opportunities because you can't fund them.

In today's economic climate, capital planning has never been more important. And it has never felt more impossible.

How about you? Do you know where the capital would come from if you needed cash to keep the doors open until a big client pays up? Or maybe you've had to lay off so many people that you struggle to serve the clients who still rely on you, much less being able to muster the resources to serve new prospects that come knocking on your door. Do you have a plan for getting your hands on cash to retool as your industry changes?

Maybe your capital plan works like this: *I'll figure it out.* Or, *I've always been able to get by.* Or, *I just won't take any money out.*

Some of us leave to chance our big-picture strategy for the capital needs of our business. Or we think we can carry it on our own backs long enough for the business to start clicking. We think if working hard isn't working, we'll just work harder.

Here are three questions you can ask yourself right now to evaluate your present level of capital strategy.

Lifeblood Plus

Capital **partners** aren't a prerequisite for business wealth. Capital **planning** is.

1. Have you intentionally identified resources you can tap for capital when the company needs more than you can fund with its monthly revenue?

2. Are you deliberately protecting and preserving those resources?

3. Will you recognize and respond to the moment in the life of your business when the equity value of the company is at stake?

Let's say the answer to those questions is "no."

No, you don't have a capital strategy, but with enough shoulder to the wheel, the money will take care of itself.

The belief that the money will somehow take care of itself if you only work hard enough is reckless denial in an unstable economy. The 99% perspiration theory of success sounds good. But don't let all that sweat pouring off your forehead blind you to the need for a plan to keep the lifeblood of the business flowing when the need is critical.

Here are the truths the Asset Builder lives by:

- Most highly successful enterprises reach a point when they need capital beyond the resources of ownership if they are to achieve stable and/or significant equity value.

- The smart business owner plans for the day when the business will need more capital.

- The resulting capital plan empowers owners to achieve their economic objectives.

The Owner's Voice

"Knowing that banks are difficult, I am focused on creating a history of profitability."

The true Asset Builder understands the difference between an asset and an idea, as well as a keen sense of the relationship between risk and the need for capital. One of the tendencies that makes owners unattractive to outside capitalists is our tendency to grossly understate the risk in our untested assumptions.

A tale of two owners

Listen to how the situation played out between the two owners I wrote about at the beginning of this chapter.

One owner has been cautious about investing in the business, as well as careful about preserving his personal estate. When the need for cash arose, he was reluctant to risk his personal estate or the annual distributions he'd been receiving each year as an equity owner of a professional services firm.

The second owner had much the same attitude, until he learned the principles of the Asset Builder. When he did, he saw that he and his partner were in danger of starving the business if they didn't reinvest in it, becoming the capitalist to their enterprise during a stressed economy.

As close as brothers, the two partners could not resolve their differences.

Lifeblood Plus

Power Shift

When a bank is soliciting a business owner, the owner has the power. When the owner attempts to go after the bank, the banker has the power. Take control of the power before that shift occurs.

The first owner, the reluctant investor, ultimately bought out the owner who wanted to reinvest some of the dividends the business had paid them in the years when it was flush with profit.

The reluctant investor ended up putting his estate on the line anyway, in order to walk away with full ownership. He could easily have ended up cash-strapped

and in need of an infusion of capital.
But in recognizing that he now owns
the whole problem of cashflowing the
day-to-day needs of the business, his
mindset about the money of the
business shifted dramatically. He
focused quickly on generating new

revenue and rebuilding the cost structure of the business, including variable-
based pay that set in motion the exodus of key players who were overpaid
and under-performing. He finished his first year as sole owner with a solid
profit and a plan that should enable him to pay out his former partner over
three years—two years ahead of schedule.

His former partner has started fresh, launching a small, quirky firm
that is presently working collaboratively with other solopreneurs to develop
a product that could revolutionize personal transportation in developing
countries. He's enthusiastic and energized by the work. And it doesn't hurt
that the money he made when he sold his half of the original firm to his
founding partner has given him enough wiggle room, financially, to follow
his passion as a You, Inc.

Fairy tale endings aren't commonplace in any economy, but the
stories of these two owners show how the principles of the Asset Builder

Lifeblood Plus

Grim Fairy Tales

Three prevalent myths have grown up around the notion of outside capital.

1. All capitalists are predators.
2. Accepting outside capital is a sign of weakness.
3. Giving up equity means the owner has less.

These are **myths**. Don't fall for them.

Here's one truth: To have a healthy business, you must have a healthy relationship with capital...even if you're the investor.

Lifeblood Plus

Benefits of a Capital Plan

- You share the burden.
- You can multiply wealth.
- You're motivated to succeed.
- You're empowered to get more of what you want out of business ownership.

can work even in significantly different circumstances.

An asset in your portfolio

One of the biggest mistakes I've seen coming back to haunt owners in recent years is a classic mistake that no investor would ever make: They've built their portfolio on one investment.

If we are truly thinking like a capitalist when it comes to our business, we would never risk all of our available capital on one investment opportunity. We would know better. We would diversify.

But we have chosen, instead, to fund our business as if it defines us and our self-worth. We sometimes choose to keep funding it the way some families shore up a ne'er-do-well brother, betting the family savings that this time he's going to hit it big.

That's not thinking like a capitalist.

Yes, our business grows out of our core purpose, but the business itself is not our core purpose. It is an expression of who we are, but it does not define who we are. It's built on a vision, but the business is merely the vehicle for achieving the vision.

So our task is to balance that vision and purpose with the objective clarity of a capitalist.

When we can do that, we have paved the way for something far greater than a vehicle for earning money. We have laid the groundwork for our legacy.

Relationships, options and leverage

What exactly is a capital plan?

It is **not** knowing years in advance how much capital we'll need and marking it on the calendar so we don't miss the deadline. Business changes too fast and too frequently for that to be possible. Capital planning starts with staying attuned to the business and its needs, including calculations about what those needs will be in future *stages* of the business. Before the hawk in us begins to hunt opportunities for capital, we cultivate the eagle eye that sees the big picture of the enterprise's needs in the months and years ahead, long before the business is hungry for capital.

Step by step, here's what capital planning looks like.

1. Make the Big Decision. Owners with a capital plan have made the decision to place the needs of the business ahead of their own immediate needs. They realize they are growing an asset with its own needs,

---

Lifeblood Plus

The Price of No Capital Plant

Suppose you don't have a capital plan. Here are some possible consequences:

- You keep running out of cash, even though your financials tell you you're profitable. You keep asking, "Where did all the money go?"

- You need a little extra capital, but without planning, it's hard to get your hands on it.

- Organic growth is slower because resources are more limited.

- Momentum may be lost, which often means you miss opportunities.

- The control is all yours. So is the risk. You may miss opportunities because of lower risk tolerance.

- Some windows of opportunity may close permanently.

- The needs of a maturing business may not be fully met with limited resources.

The price of having no capital plan could be finding yourself on the cusp of significant expansion with no way to seize it. The price of those missed opportunities could be lost revenue. The price of lost revenue could be the risk of losing key players who can't defer forever and decide to look for greener pastures. The ultimate price of having no capital plan could be that there is no end in sight to your time on the treadmill.

Only you can weigh whether those trade-offs are worth the control you hang onto because your only capital plan was to dig deeper into your own pockets.

---

its own life stages of growth and needs that are separate from the needs of the owner—needs that must be met if the business is to thrive.

2. Leverage the vision. Bankers and other capitalists have made it clear that they aren't impressed by—or motivated to invest in—our vision. Don't make the mistake of thinking that means vision is no longer important. Right now, the world is aching for more vision, not less. Grandiose dreams get categorized quickly as not credible. But dreams that are energetic, that have a good sense of concrete plan as their foundation, still give people hope.

Lifeblood Plus

Potential Payoffs of Capital Planning

Capital partners aren't for everyone. But what if you'd made the choice to devise a capital strategy that created the right kind of capital for the right moment in the life of your business? What might that look like?

- You have multiple capital options, including a number of banks and potential investors. With so many options, you're able to structure the best terms.

- Cash on hand and cash reserves are healthy.

- Early-stage employees begin to see the rewards, and their commitment deepens.

- You've established true market value and equity value for your company.

- If you chose investors as part of your capital plan, you now have additional stakeholders who are committed to helping you succeed.

- You've elevated your accountability for success to your stockholders, including yourself.

- The risk is no longer all on your shoulders.

- You ride the momentum to the next life stage of your business.

Lifeblood Plus

Different species of capitalists

Self-funders: Many early-stage entrepreneurs shoulder the whole burden. The idea of reaping all the rewards while controlling your own destiny has appeal. This is sometimes offset by a very real downside: The risk is high and yours alone. And the rewards may be limited or very long in coming because there is less capital to fund growth. What the self-funder wants: Control.

Friends & family: This is one of the most common sources of investment capital, but one that offers big potential for entanglements. Be careful: No business is worth the cost of friends and the love of family. If you go this route, spell out all the conditions and expectations clearly and often. Make sure your investors know every dollar could be lost and how long it might be before they could see a return. For yourself, be very clear about any expectations that may come with the investment; some friends and family may feel their investment gives them say-so about how that money is used. Spell it out, for everyone's sake. What friends and family want: To not lose their shirts.

Lenders: Commercial banks and other lenders are a type of capitalist who could play key roles at pivotal moments in your game. This is the best-priced capital in town. What the lender wants: A sure-thing and the collateral to back it up.

Venture Capitalists: This isn't for everyone. But when you find yourself moving toward a golden opportunity that will need resources outside the comfort zone of traditional lenders, the right venture capitalists can be true strategic partners and a key component in the Asset Builder's capital plan. If that kind of opportunity fits your vision, it may be wise to cultivate these relationships long before the need arises. What venture capitalists want: significant reward in proportion with their risk and a specific plan for exiting the business with that reward; often, they also enjoy participation in the success of high-potential opportunities.

Vulture Capitalists: These are the last-resort guys who move in for the kill when companies have run out of options. What the vulture capitalist wants: To grab a dying business for next to nothing.

3. Take the necessary steps to become investor-ready.
Investors like systems-driven businesses with leaders focused on repeatable actions that give profitable results. That's the essence of being investor-ready in today's marketplace.

4. Cultivate capital sources. Smart Money owners cultivate relationships with people who are potential beneficiaries of the success of their businesses. These are people who are looking for ways to multiply their own money. Build these relationships now, not when you need the money. The best relationships are cultivated for years before an investment is needed. These are the true investors who desire mutual success, not a chance to pick the bones.

5. Diversify fund sources. Create as many different avenues and options as possible for getting your hands on cash. Whenever possible, make sure the most accessible source is also the lowest-cost source of backup money.

Core competency

In that context, what exactly is a capital plan?

A capital plan is what differentiates the business owner whose business doesn't survive him from the one who has created a sustainable asset with sufficient capital to grow through its life stages.

Developing a capital plan is a big leap from the simple starting point of learning to earn and keeping your eyes on the money. Every Smart Money Rule challenges business owners, no matter what the life stage of their business, to think differently about money and to treat it differently.

But capital planning is a notch above all the others. Capital planning distinctly separates those who want to build an asset with significant value. When you take this step, you are moving into territory that only a small percentage of business owners ever reach.

The territory of the Business Asset Builder is ripe for conquering. Making the move requires commitment and courage, but I don't know a

133

true entrepreneur who doesn't have both. And now you have the rules of the road.

Any business owner, any time, can answer the call.

Ownership Perspective

1. Have you ever experienced that gut wrenching moment of "no confidence" from your banker (who you thought was a trusted friend to your business)? How has that affected you today in the way you plan for the capital needs of your company?

2. Have you ever lost a significant wealth opportunity for your business because you did not have the capital on hand to seize the moment?

3. Is it difficult for you accept that you may need others to invest in your business for it to realize its fullest potential? And that to do so means that you create an asset that you share with others while, likely, making yourself wealthier?

The Asset Builder's Code:

Owners cannot transform their businesses without transforming themselves.

CHAPTER TWELVE
IT'S FUNDAMENTAL:
A LEGACY OF HOPE

"Nothing speaks as loudly for freedom as the entrepreneurial spirit."

The Great Recession has changed everything. People who are waiting for a return to the kind of economy we experienced before the meltdown are deceiving themselves.

If that's so, does it mean we're stuck in the grinding job called Business Ownership, with its countless responsibilities and shrinking rewards?

No. Far from it. I see plenty of reasons for hope in the future. And one of them is found in our shift in focus from business ownership as a vehicle for getting rich to ownership as an expression of our purpose or deeper significance.

Recently, my younger daughter, Molly, was assigned to interview and write about a business owner as part of her studies at Auburn University. She chose to write about my journey as a business owner. By phone, she interviewed me to fill in the details of a story she knew from hearing bits and pieces of it throughout her childhood. Then she sat up late into the evening, writing the story of her dad's ownership journey.

The fact that Molly is my daughter and that the subject is me has nothing to do with the fact that the paper she wrote for class was brilliantly good and moving in its insights.

Or maybe the truth is that Molly's paper was brilliant in spite of her subject matter.

Whatever the case, here is what I saw in my 22-year-old daughter's paper: It is one mark of the legacy I have been building during my quarter-century of business ownership, a story for my children and their children and their children.

Getting glimpses

When I first started my consulting firm and the Institute about 20 years ago, my statement of purpose read like this: To invest in great leaders for the Kingdom on the platform of private enterprise.

Grandiose? Maybe. Personally, I think any vision worth its salt should be a little bit grandiose. If it's not, why not just schlep to work every day, punch a time clock and put on a uniform or step into a cubicle?

I would say I worked to stay in my vision and purpose I claimed for myself, but it is ultimately the generations that follow us who will declare our legacy. Most of us will only get glimpses of our legacy when our daughters write about us for a college paper; when our sons come to work for us and have that first flash of understanding about what we've been doing to put food on the table for decades; when a leader we've nurtured tells us about a turning-point moment.

In those glimpses, I believe, lies our hope for the future.

Rich or wealthy?

I was never satisfied just to be rich. How about you?

For some of us, learning to play by Smart Money Rules gives us our best shot at becoming rich. For those of us who persevere, playing by Smart

Money Rules could get us off the treadmill someday. Certainly it could mean that we won't be sweating bullets over payroll, although the big growth moves might still give us a few knots in the stomach. It's more likely that we'll be able to do what we like best inside our business more often. Maybe we'll begin to feel that we've earned a degree

of the freedom and autonomy we've always dreamed of. Maybe we'll see the day on the horizon when we can hand over the reins to the next generation, either to our own children or to the leaders we've raised up in the business. Or maybe you're that breed of entrepreneur who is always hungry to create and innovate, either by starting another business or becoming a capitalist to other enterprise builders.

Any of those achievements could be an expression of wealth as we define it for ourselves.

However we define it, most of us have a deep desire to build something significant. We want to see the summit beyond this summit, and conquer it, too. Remember our pioneer legacy? We're descended from pioneers, from bold adventurers who conquered a wilderness. People who still feel that spirit and answer the call of an entrepreneurial revolution won't be satisfied with counting the money.

Those of us with the deepest well of pioneer spirit want to build something that outlives us, something that wouldn't have existed without us. To achieve that, we must never let today's economic circumstances rob us of our hope.

I've seen so many remarkable successes in the midst of the pain of the last few years. For myself, I've taken this opportunity to build an electronic library of my writings and make it available to business owners over the Internet at SamFrowine.com.

I've seen successful owners become better leaders to their enterprises as they grew in humility and gave up some attachments. Some, I've seen crushed.

I've seen the entrepreneurial spirit coming alive in my children as they've realized that jobs aren't guaranteed to anyone, even college graduates.

I've seen owners who have recognized that their legacy may be different from what they imagined, but their work still has legacy value.

Lifeblood Plus

The Four Stages of Business Ownership

Stage 1: You, Inc. We have an idea, find a way to finance it and reach an audience. The business is wrapped around us as we move through start-up and launch, astounding everyone when we reach the low six figures. Maybe we're content to be solopreneurs or maybe we've found and inspired a few loyal people eager for the punishment of pulling the plow of a would-be enterprise. About all we have is a dream, but it's enough to keep us going when the bank statement looks pretty scary. The majority of businesses never make it past this point. We either go under or settle into a one-person-shop existence that never makes us rich but still feels satisfying on some levels. We encounter a Smart Money Rule from time to time, but don't understand them well enough yet to follow them consistently. Success is measured by revenue.

Stage 2: Owner Asset Builder. The business is taking shape, building systems and procedures and customer base. We run the show until the pace and the pressure make it impossible to do everything ourselves. A few leaders begin to grow up around us and gain our confidence and, in some cases, we begin to release responsibility into their hands. The business will break into seven figures, but how big the numbers get is in direct proportion to how willing we are to step back and give our leaders real authority. Time and again, we hit a ceiling of complexity and exhaustion that we break through only by handing off the reins to others. Some Smart Money owners stop here, unable or unwilling to move beyond this point. Success is measured by earnings.

Stage 3: Owner Capitalist. Leaders run the show. We've settled into a role that takes full advantage of our unique contribution to the business. We feel

I find great hope in knowing that the fundamentals endure and that part of our legacy can be found in how we apply the fundamentals.

Challenges of the journey

I also find hope in recognizing that these challenges we face are part of our journey.

Those who don't understand that business ownership is a journey like to think that our success is a combination of luck and savvy. But even

---

relief from stepping off the treadmill although the periodic crisis takes us back a step or two. Smart Money Rules are second nature to us and to our leaders, so revenue is consistently good, profit is reliable. Our leaders are reaping rewards, as well. Re-investing in the business has resulted in a valuable asset and our personal portfolio is healthy. Even so, we're developing more than one source of capital in case it's needed. But we're beginning to get restless. Our entrepreneurial spirit is getting tired of the status quo. Without wise counsel, we might buy a boat or stir things up and make moves just because we need a little adventure. This is when ill-considered acquisitions or expansions or other growth moves can cripple a thriving enterprise. Success is measured in equity value.

Stage 4: Enterprise Investor. The ultimate Asset Builder, we've secured our finances both personally and inside the business. We saw this day coming and we've positioned ourselves to use a percentage of company profits as working capital outside the business. Our enterprise has become the ultimate wealth machine, where money begets money. We may or may not sell the original enterprise, but we steward our resources well. We satisfy our entrepreneurial spirit by supporting the growth of other young enterprises through angel investment and sometimes with our hard-earned wisdom. We can see countless new summits from where we stand and we are prepared to conquer them. We can select the challenges that are most meaningful to us. We have the best of all possible worlds: *We have enough money and enough freedom to pursue whatever frontiers our spirit craves.* Success is measured in portfolio wealth and in the intangibles I think of as True Wealth—family, faith, stewardship, peace of mind.

---

today, as so much seems out of our control, our end journey is a by-product of our choices. When we understand the choices and make them consciously, we have more control of our own destiny.

One of those choices is the critical choice to operate from Smart Money Rules and to shift our thinking to embrace the Asset Builder's Code. Whether you're currently a You, Inc., or an Asset Builder, you'll know you're on this journey when you accept the challenges to:

1. Treat your business like a valuable asset. The owner is more than an executive leader, more than a manager, more than the big boss. At the top of every company is the one person who sets the tone for the organization by treating the business like a valuable asset. That person is the owner.

2. Face the inner enemies. If owners set the tone in their companies, they must face their enemies—especially the ones that implicate them. They must become accountable for their entitlement mentality, their fears, the sacred cows that impact the entire organization and keep them from making wise choices that protect the business asset.

The Owner's Voice

"After the Big Re-Set, my personal income dropped significantly, and I evaluated working somewhere else as a 'safe harbor.' However, I realize there is no such thing, and certainly no safe harbor that values my personal freedom as much as I do. With that in mind, owning your own business is the only true safe harbor for what matters—personal freedom—and the greatest hope of economic freedom."

3. Treat the money of the business like oxygen to the brain. It's vital to survival. It makes everything else work. When it's gone, it's game over.

4. Pursue the extraordinary. Plenty of owners desire greatness; few have the gumption to go for it. The world needs dreamers because dreams give us hope and hope enriches our lives in countless ways.

5. Seek wise counsel. Entrepreneurs can think so expansively and so out-of-the-box that they're vulnerable to blowing things up. That's why it's invaluable to leverage the experience and insights of those who are farther along in their journeys.

Becoming an Asset Builder requires hard choices that go beyond the actions we take with our money. Becoming the Asset Builder affects the beliefs and values that underpin our use of money.

As we shift our beliefs about success, we also begin to make different choices about the way we live our lives. We adopt the mind-set of the steward who neither hoards nor squanders, but puts his resources to work in service to a higher calling. We understand what it means to place our personal desires behind the needs of our enterprise, our family, our community.

A hero for the revolution

Greg Crumpton became one of my heroes in the entrepreneurial revolution. He epitomizes a shifting world view.

An engineer by training, Greg owns a full-service HVAC and mechanical contracting company that specializes in Computer Room Environmental Systems design, installation and maintenance for temperature-sensitive environments. He is deeply committed to the people of his organization and their success.

Because of his success, he was targeted for roll-up by a national company ten times larger than his own. The offer was good—very good, actually—and it came with the opportunity for Greg to continue as leader of the enterprise and IPO potential in the not-too-distant future. The opportunity was right.

But when decision-time rolled around, Greg found himself wrestling with the question we should all wrestle with at different junctures in the life of our enterprises: What mattered most to him?

When he asked the question, his answer became clear. What mattered most to Greg was a legacy that would allow the people in his enterprise to fulfill the vision they had committed to together. The company was family to Greg. He realized that he would never regret the decision in this season to stick with his people, deliver great service and grow together.

With all the economic scarcity around us, Greg chose the thing that matters most to him. He chose a different kind of wealth.

You can see why he is one of my heroes.

Never too late

Each of us plays the game in our own way. We get to choose our own playing field. We get to choose our own scoring criteria. We even get to make up our own rules, if that's the way we choose to play the game. After all, that's why we're entrepreneurs, isn't it?

But no matter where you are in the game of your business, it's never too late to change your rules. As long as there's a dollar in the bank, it's never too late to start playing by Smart Money Rules. It's never too late to start reaping the benefits of following the Asset Builder's Code.

The catch is that it isn't just about the money.

Money is the lifeblood, it's true. Mastering the practices that protect the lifeblood of our enterprise is a basic, a pre-requisite for success.

But mastering the game calls on us to radically redefine ourselves as business owners.

It calls on us to change our beliefs and values, to confront our fears, to dig deep for our true motives and purpose. It calls on us to change deeply and profoundly.

A stake in the ground

We've all been given a wake-up call. For decades, we've taken for granted this land of milk and honey that is America's social and economic landscape. It's been a given that we could achieve more than our parents achieved, that the sky's the limit for people who work hard and make all the right moves, that we are a measuring stick for the world.

In taking those things for granted, we've exposed our arrogance. And in the fallout from the shift that has taken place here, our vulnerability has also been exposed.

The first edition of **_Lifeblood_** closed with a call to action, a vision for the pinnacle of wealth where owners could see that their opportunities were limitless. Few of us feel we're anywhere close to a pinnacle like that today. We've been humbled and, yes, in many cases humiliated, by the vice grip of the economic shift.

But the challenge remains.

We can step into our roles as the pioneers who will reshape our world for the 21st Century. We can carve new pathways into the wilderness for the next generation of entrepreneurs. We can leave the breadcrumbs of our mistakes for them to follow to better ideas than we can imagine from where we stand today. We can shine the light across a landscape that will be its own place of milk and honey.

And we can put a stake in the ground for freedom.

Nothing speaks as loudly for freedom as the entrepreneurial spirit. It is the spirit of innovation and creativity and hope for something better. It is the spirit of courage and enthusiasm and opportunity that lifts our communities.

That's our collective legacy, as entrepreneurs.

When you protect the lifeblood resources that keep your business healthy, that's what you're protecting: our economic freedom and our legacy to future generations.

Ownership Perspective

1. Do you clearly understand the difference between the views of the "rich" business owner versus the "wealthy" one? Which do you aspire to be?

2. If you have chosen the Asset Builder journey, which stage are you in right now—Entrepreneur, CEO, Owner Capitalist or Enterprise Investor?

3. What will you have to give up in the way of habits and choices to embrace the challenge of becoming a true Asset Builder? If you intentionally engage in this True Wealth journey, what rewards can you expect?

4. How does this business carry on without you? What is your succession plan?

Appendix

The Asset Builder's Code

For almost two decades, Sam has been refining and integrating the best practices of highly successful business owners into a body of knowledge for business owners who desire to become Asset Builders. This body of knowledge has become the **Business Asset Builder's Code**.

The Code is based on the hard-earned wisdom of experienced business owners who have contributed to the depth and breadth of the body of knowledge that makes up the Code. And in today's economy, it is applicable to any enterprise, from You, Inc., to the builders of major enterprises.

I. Lifeblood is found in the relationship between time and money: Healthy and rhythmic cash flow buys time to refine the success formula of the business.

II. The only person with the authority, the accountability and the unique perspective to build and cultivate the business as an asset with market value is the owner.

III. Every decision, every choice, impacts the lifeblood of the business.

IV. Making money is hard; hanging onto it is even harder.

V. Asset Builders balance the need to survive the day with the importance of keeping an eye on the future.

VI. Business is a living organism; the lifeblood that sustains it must be protected.

VII. The vision of building a meaningful legacy unlocks the economic potential of an enterprise.

VIII. Owners cannot transform their businesses without transforming themselves.

IX. Asset Builders ingrain the principles of economic health deep in the DNA of their organizations.

X. Investing in the business creates equity appreciation; expenses are non-recoverable and represent lost liquidity.

XI. The highest stage of enterprise building is converting company profits into a source of capital used to create a continuous stream of revenue independent of the entrepreneur's involvement.

XII. Business owners get rich by building rich relationships. Rich relationships are the True Wealth of ownership.

The Language of the Asset Builder

Sam developed the Asset Builder's Code and the Enterprise Builder System over the course of more than two decades in the laboratory of ownership. Some of his language is unique to the practices and beliefs that make up the Code and the System.

Business Asset Builder
The business owner who aspires to build a healthy enterprise that treats the business and its equity like valuable stock

Crossroads
Critical junctures in the life of business owners who are transitioning from their role in an owner-centered entrepreneurial pursuit to their new role in a leader-centered enterprise with financial sustainability

Entrepreneurial Revolution
Dominance of successful private enterprise as the driving force behind economic health in the 21st-century; the spirit that drives this revolution may go dormant but it will not go away as long as the entrepreneurial spirit is driven by the desire to seek freedom

Grand Vision
Ownership's picture of how the business will look, feel and function when it has achieved a certain level of success that is linked to ownership's greater purpose for the enterprise

Great Enterprise
A sustainable wealth-generating machine that is legacy-bound and centers on the right values and a sense of contribution to society or the world

Lifeblood
The resources of time, money and people that enable a business to sustain, allowing the enterprise to become a Great Enterprise and achieve the owner's wealth objectives

True Wealth

The state of mind and spirit that occurs when people use their talent and their passion to gain deep satisfaction from work that is significant in its contribution value not only to ownership but to all those it touches

You, Inc.

A new breed of owners of microenterprises, often established based on a specific skill set, talent or passion; the purpose at the core of all entrepreneurs and the businesses they found; the language is found in hundreds of books and articles and origin of the term is unknown, but the concept is foundational to Asset Builder principles

Sam's Bookshelf

Asset Builders learn, adapt and grow continuously. They are thinking people who remain open to new ideas and new perspectives. Reading allows business owners to tap the best thinking in the world as a way to improve their enterprise-building skills. These are a few of Sam's favorite reads, books that have had a powerful influence on the way he thinks and acts on his ownership journey. They're categorized here around four key concepts of Wealth Building.

Thinking Like a Wealth Builder

Allen, James, *As a Man Thinketh.* Barnes and Noble, Inc., early 1900s.

Boulton, Richard E.S., Barry D. Libert, and Steve M. Samek. *Cracking the Value Code: How Successful Businesses Are Creating Wealth in the New Economy.* New York: HarperCollins, 2000.

Brush, C.G.; N.M. Carter; E.J. Gatewood; P.G. Greene; M. Hart, *Insight Report, Women business owners and equity capital: The myths dispelled,* Kansas City, MO: Kauffman Center for Entrepreneurial Leadership, Marion Ewing Kauffman Foundation.

Brush, Candida; Nancy M. Carter; Elizabeth Gatewood; Patricia G. Greene; and Myra M. Hart, *Clearing the Hurdles: Women Building High-Growth Businesses.* Prentice-Hall, 2004.

Collins, Jim, *Good to Great: Why Some Companies Make the Leap…and Others Don't.* Harper Business, 2001.

Costa, Rebecca D., *The Watchman's Rattle: Thinking Our Way Out of Extinction.* Vangaurd Press, 2010.

Covey, Stephen R., *First Things First.* Simon and Schuster, 1995.

Crosson, Russ, *A Life Well Spent: The Eternal Rewards of Investing Yourself and Your Money in Your Family.* Ronald Blue and Company, LLC, 1994.

Csikszentmihalyi, Mihalyi, *Flow: The Psychology of Optimal Experience.* New York: Harper Collins Publishers, 1990.

Csikszentmihalyi, Mihaly, *Good Business: Leadership, Flow, and the Making of Meaning.* Viking, published by The Penguin Group, 2003.

Douglas, Deborah, *Ripe: Harvesting the Value of Your Business.* New York: Select Books, Inc., 2010.

Drucker, Peter, *The Age of Discontinuity: Guidelines for Our Changing Society.* Harper and Roe, Publishers, 1968.

Fox, Jeffrey J., *How to Make Big Money in Your Own Small Business.* New York: Hyperion, 2004.

Frankl, Viktor, *Man's Search for Meaning: An Introduction to Logotherapy.* Boston: Beacon Press, 1959. 154.

Gladwell, Malcolm, *Blink.* New York: Back Bay Books/ Little, Brown and Company, 2005.

Gladwell, Malcolm, *Outliers: The Story of Success.* New York: Little, Brown and Company, 2008.

Godin, Seth, *Purple Cow: Transform Your Business by Being Remarkable.* Portfolio, a Member of Penguin Group (USA), Inc., 2003.

Goldratt, Eliyahu, and Jeff Cox, *The Goal.* Great Barrington, MA: North River Press, 1992.

Hall, Doug and David Wecker, *The Maverick Mindset: Finding the Courage to Journey from Fear to Freedom.* Simon and Schuster, 1997.

Hamel, Gary, *Leading the Revolution.* New York: Penguin Group, 2002. Rev. ed.

Handy, Charles, *Waiting for the Mountain to Move: Reflecting on Work and Life.* San Francisco: Jossey-Bass Publishers, 1999.

Harnish, Verne, *Mastering the Rockefeller Habits: What You Must Do to Increase the Value of Your Fast Growth Firm.* SelectBooks, Inc., 2002.

Heath, Chip & Dan, *Switch: How To Change Things When Change is Hard.* New York: Broadway Books, 2010.

Lencioni, Patrick, *The Five Temptations of a CEO.* Jossey-Bass Publishers, 1998.

Ries, Al, *Focus: The Future of Your Company Depends on It.* Harper Business, 1996.

Robbins, Anthony, *Awaken the Giant Within.* Free Press, 1992.

Senge, Peter, *The Fifth Discipline: The Art and Practice of the Learning Organization.* New York: Doubleday Currency, 1994.

Tracy, Brian, *Change Your Thinking, Change Your Life.* John Wylie and Sons, Inc., 2003.

Tracy, Brian, *Focal Point: A Proven System to Simplify Your Life, Double Your Productivity, and Achieve All Your Goals.* New York: AMACOM-American Management Association, 2001.

Tracy, Brian, *Goals! How to Get Everything You Want Faster Than You Ever Thought Possible.* San Francisco: Berrett-Koehler, 2003.

Managing Lifeblood: Time, Money and People

Adler, Lou, *Hire with Your Head.* Hoboken, NJ: John Wiley & Sons, 1998.

Godin, Seth, *Tribes.* New York: Penguin Group, 2008.

Goldsmith, Marshall, *Succession: Are You Ready?* Boston: Harvard Business School Publishing, 2009.

Kiyosaki, Robert T. with Sharon L. Lechter., CPA, *Rich Dad's Cashflow Quadrant.* Warner Business Books, 1998.

Kiyosaki, Robert T. with Sharon L. Lechter, CPA, *Rich Dad's Guide to Investing: What the Rich Invest In that the Poor and the Middle Class Do Not!* Warner Business Books, 2000.

Kiyosaki, Robert T. with Sharon L. Lechter, CPA, *Rich Kid, Smart Kid: Give Your Child a Financial Headstart.* Warner Business Books, 2001.

Kiyosaki, Robert T. with Sharon L. Lechter, CPA, *Rich Dad's Prophesy: Why the Biggest Stock Market Crash in History is Still Coming…and How You Can Prepare Yourself and Profit from It!* Warner Business Books, 2002.

Lencioni, Patrick, *The Five Dysfunctions of a Team.* Jossey-Bass Publishers, 2002.

Masterson, Michael, *Automatic Wealth, The Six Steps to Financial Independence.* 2005.

Pilzer, Paul Zane, *Unlimited Wealth: The Theory and Practice of Economic Alchemy.* Crown, 1991.

Stanley, Thomas J., Ph.D., *The Millionaire Mind.* Andrews McMeel Publishing, 2000.

Ramsey, Dave, *EntreLeadership: 20 Years of Practical Business Wisdom from the Trenches.* New York: Howard Books, 2011.

Tracy, Brian, *Getting Rich Your Own Way: Achieve All Your Financial Goals Faster than You Ever Thought Possible.* John Wiley and Sons, Inc., 2004.

Strategies for Building Great Enterprise

Anderson, Dave, *Up Your Business! Seven Steps to Fix, Build, or Stretch Your Organization.* John Wiley and Sons, Inc., 2003.

Bhide, A., *The Origin and Evolution of New Businesses.* New York: Oxford University Press, 2000.

Brafman, Ori and Rod A Beckstrom, *The Starfish and the Spider: The Unstoppable Power of the Leaderless Organizations.* New York: Penguin Group, 2006.

Brandt, Steven C., *Entrepreneuring: The Ten Commandments for Building a Growth Company.* Massachusetts: Addison-Wesley Publishing Company, 1983.

Brandt, Steven C., *Focus Your Business: Strategic Planning in Emerging Companies.* Friday Harbor, WA: Archipelago Publishing, 1997.

Cohn, Theodore and Roy A. Lindberg, *Survival and Growth (Management Strategies for the Small Firm.* New York: AMACOM, a Division of American Management Associations, 1978.

Drucker, Peter, *Managing for Results: Economic Tasks and Risk-Taking Decision.* New York: HarperBusiness, 1993.

Drucker, Peter, *Innovation and Entrepreneurship.* New York: Harper-Business, 1999.

Fox, Jeffrey J., *How To Be a Fierce Competitor: What Winning Companies and Great Managers Do in Tough Times.* San Francisco: Jossey-Bass Publishers, 2010.

Fried, Jason and David Heinemeier Hansson, *Rework.* New York: Crown Publishing Group, 2010.

Gerber, Michael E., *The E Myth Revisited: Why Most Businesses Don't Work and What to Do About It.* Harper Business, 1995.

Gerber, Michael E., *E Myth Mastery: The Seven Essential Disciplines for Building a World Class Company.* Harper Business, 2005.

Kaplan, Robert S., and David P. Norton, *The Balanced Scorecard: Translating*

Strategy Into Action. Boston: Harvard Business School Press, 1996.

Kim, W. Chan and Renée Mauborgne, *Blue Ocean Strategy: How to Create Uncontested Market Space and Make the Competition Irrelevant.* Harvard Business School Publishing Corporation, 2005.

Lonier, Terri, *Smart Strategies for Growing Your Business.* John Wylie and Sons, Inc., 1999.

Treacy, Michael and Fred Wiersma, *The Discipline of Market Leaders: Choose Your Customers, Narrow Your Focus, Dominate Your Market.* Reading, MA: Addison-Wesley, 1997.

Leadership Wisdom

Time with God: The New Testament for Busy People. Word Publishing Inc. 1991.

Batterson, Mark, *The Circle Maker: Praying Circles Around Your Biggest Dreams and Greatest Fears.* Austin: Fedd & Company. Inc., 2011.

Bennis, Warren, *On Becoming a Leader.* New York: Perseus Publishing, 1994.

Blackaby, Henry and Richard, *Spiritual Leadership: Moving People on to God's Agenda.* Nashville: Broadman & Holman Publishers, 2001.

Catlin, Katherine and Jana Matthews, *Leading at the Speed of Growth: Journey from Entrepreneur to CEO.* Hungry Minds, Inc., 2001, Kauffman Center for Entrepenurial Leadership, Marion Ewing Kauffman Foundation.

Dormann, Henry O. *Letters from Leaders: Personal Advice for Tomorrow's Leaders from the World's Most Influential People.* The Globe Pequot Press, 2009.

Drucker, Peter, *The Effective Executive.* Harper and Roe, 1966, 1967.

Grayling, A. C., *Ideas that Matter: The Concpets that Shape the 21st Century.* New York: Perseus Books Group, 2010.

Keller, Timothy. *Counterfeit Gods: The Empty Promises of Money, Sex, and Power, and the Only Hope That Matters.* New York: Penguin Group, 2009.

Maxwell, John C., *Developing the Leaders Around You.* Thomas Nelson Publishers, 1995.

Maxwell, John C., *The 21 Irrefutable Laws of Leadership.* Nashville: Thomas Nelson, 1998.

Maxwell, John C., *Thinking for a Change.* Warner Books, 2003.

Miller, Donald, *A Million Miles in a Thousand Years.* Nashville: Thomas Nelson, Inc., 2009.

Moreland, J.P., *Love Your God with all Your Mind: The Role of Reason in the Life of the Soul.* Colorado Springs: NavPress, 1997.

Patterson, Kerry, Joseph Grenny, David Maxfield, Ron McMillan, and Al Switzler. *Influencer: The Power to Change Anything.* New York: McGraw Hill, 2008.

Peters, Tom, *The Little Big Things: 163 Ways to Pursue Excellence.* New York: HarperCollins Publishers, 2010.

Phillips, Donald T., *Lincoln on Leadership.* New York: Warner, 1992.

Sanders, Tim, *The Likeability Factor: How To Boost Your L-Factor & Achieve Your Life's Dreams.* New York: Random House, Inc., 2005.

Whitney, David C., and Robin Vaughn Whitney. *The American Presidents: Biographies of the Chief Executives from George Washington through Barack Obama.* 11th Edition. The Reader's Digest Association, Inc., 2009.

Zadra, Dan, and Susan Scott. *Brilliance: Uncommon Voices from Uncommon Women.* Seattle: Compendium, 2010.

Made in the USA
Charleston, SC
20 February 2013